9/80 8

D1154878

Seaweeds

Seaweeds

A Color-Coded, Illustrated Guide
to Common Marine Plants
of the East Coast of the United States

C. J. Hillson

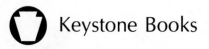 Keystone Books

The Pennsylvania State University Press
University Park and London

Library of Congress Cataloging in Publication Data

Hillson, Charles James, 1926-
  Seaweeds.
  Includes index and bibliography
  1. Marine algae—Atlantic coast (United States)—
Identification. 2. Marine flora—Atlantic coast
(United States)—Identification. I. Title.
QK571.5.A84H54 589.39'2'14 76—42192
ISBN 0-271-01239-0

Designed by Glenn Ruby

Printed in the United States of America

To

My wife, Patricia, whose tolerance and encouragement were a driving force, and to my teenage daughter, Carolyn, whose inability to understand why anyone would voluntarily study seaweeds was a constant challenge.

Contents

Preface

High-speed automobiles, interstate highways, shorter work weeks, longer vacations, and higher salaries have all combined to bring the seashore closer to man, wherever he lives, than ever before. Where once a visit to the shore was only a dream for many, or a once-in-a-lifetime trip for others, the varied oceanic life that has held man's interest for centuries is now just beyond the garage doors of the mobile American family. And the same curiosity that stirs the beachcombing instincts of coastal dwellers is possessed by inlanders. The difference is that for the first time a midwesterner can now do something about that curiosity. A vacation at the shore is as much within his grasp as a visit to his state capital or the nearest state park. Each year more and more inland residents are finding the coastal vacation to their liking. As a result, beachcombing is more popular than ever, with the same old questions being repeated over and over: "What's this?" "Where do you suppose that came from?" "Is that a plant or an animal?" Unfortunately, the answers in too many instances are not readily available.

This guide to the marine plants most likely to be found by the casual visitor to the Atlantic coast of the United States is written for the layman. Although there are several excellent technical books available on the subject, they are of little use to the person not familiar with botanical jargon. For one reason or another, the need for a nontechnical book on east coast seaweeds has not been satisfied. In contrast, there are several nontechnical or semitechnical books available which describe the marine flora of the west coast.

There is one notable exception to this void: *Seaweeds of Cape Cod and the Islands* by John M. Kingsbury. But since this book deals with a specific area, and quite successfully, it does not serve the same purpose this publication is designed to serve. That is, a quick reference for the identification of a particular seaweed whether the finder is in Maine, on the Delmarva Peninsula, or in Florida. Obviously, to cover such a large area many plants had to be excluded to keep the guide from being unwieldy. But those plants most likely to be found, either as drift, windrow, or attached specimens of the intertidal zone, have been included. By means of color, line drawings, and at most with the aid of a small pocket lens of no more than 10X magnification, the identification of the plant in hand, if at all common, should be possible. Seventy-nine plants are illustrated and described. As an additional help, a few of the marine animals likely to be mistaken for plants are included.

All of the illustrations in this manual were made by the author from specimens collected over the past ten years. These collections now form part of the Phycological Herbarium of The Pennsylvania State University and are permanently preserved as dried specimens, glycerin preserved whole mounts, and/or liquid preserved specimens of entire plants or portions of plants. An attempt has been made to illustrate, as often as possible, entire plants including in some instances the shell, stone, or other object to which the plant was attached. It is hoped that the illustrations will not only aid in the identification of a particular plant but will convey to the reader something of the nature of the habitat in which the plant is characteristically found.

It would be difficult to list by name all of the people who have assisted in one way or another in the preparation of this book. Although I take full responsibility for any errors which might be found, be they typographical or factual, I would be amiss not to mention certain individuals who were of special help. To Dr. Ronald A. Pursell for reading the entire manuscript, to Dr. Charles Bursey and Dr. Alice Beatty for their help with the invertebrates, and to Mrs. Gladys Marshall who patiently typed and retyped pages as I made deletions, corrections, and changes, I am greatly indebted. All are associated with The Pennsylvania State University, Department of Biology. To Dr. E.E. Webber, Keuka College, Keuka Park, New York, for reading the manuscript, to Dr. Frederick M. Bayer of the Smithsonian Institution for his help with the gorgonians and to the many students in my phycology classes and marine biology course who contributed collections and tidbits of information about individual plants, I am grateful. To the Department of Biology and The Pennsylvania State University for facilities and travel funds, I am appreciative, and to the publisher for innovative ideas and suggestions on format, appearance, and readability, I owe a great deal. Last but not least, to the workers whose publications I consulted frequently for species distributions, salient features, and specialized facts about the plants I have included herein, I give special recognition. Especially helpful were the publications of William Randolph Taylor, John M. Kingsbury, and the late E. Yale Dawson. The books written by these three outstanding phycologists, as well as the publications of others from which I gleaned specific information, are listed in the References. Some of these workers I know personally, others by name only. All of them share with me a special interest in the marine flora, and that makes us colleagues and friends as well as cohorts.

C.J.H.

Introduction

For most of us the word "weed" probably brings to mind a wayside plant of no particular merit—a dandelion in an otherwise unblemished lawn, an upstart sprig of green in the crack of a sidewalk. In other words, we tend to define a weed as an undesirable plant—a plant growing where it is not wanted, an obtrusive plant. Accordingly, a tomato plant in the middle of a corn field, no matter how productive, becomes a weed, and vice versa. A flowering plant, no matter how lovely, is a weed if it makes its appearance in a place where it is not wanted. Yet to define a weed thus presents obvious problems. A value judgment is being made and "one man's weed" might indeed be "another man's flower."

Few but professionals probably view a seaweed as anything but a weed which happens to grow in the ocean. But, as with terrestrial plants, a value judgment is being made and seaweeds, though regarded as a nuisance by most people, play an important part in the livelihood and survival of many marine organisms. In addition, some form the basis for the multimillion dollar alginate, carrageenin, and agar-agar industries. Extracts from sea-weeds produced by these industries are found in many food products which we eat daily, and in a variety of other preparations such as cosmetics, hand lotions, medications, and gels. Wherever a stabilizer or emulsifier is desirable in a product, one of the seaweed extracts is likely to be found. Thus the seaweed itself, or a derivative of it, plays an important part in our everyday world.

The Kinds of Seaweeds

Unlike the terrestrial environment where vascular plants are dominant, in the marine habitat the nonvascular plants, i.e., those without specific conducting systems, are the more abundant and conspicuous. Of these, mosses and liverworts are totally lacking and the fungi are small and inconspicuous, though apparently more abundant than once thought. Bacteria are ubiquitous but, being microscopic, are beyond the scope of this manual. The algae then, along with the few vascular plants present in the form of "grasses," there being no ferns or gymnosperms in the sea, are the plants generally referred to when the word seaweed is used. This book is about them, their identification, and the kinds most likely to be seen by the casual visitor to the beach.

What Are Algae?

Botanically, plants recognized as algae are photosynthetic organisms of simple structure which vary in size from individuals close to 300 feet in length down to single cells which can be seen only with the aid of a microscope. They are poorly differentiated plants having no leaves, stems, or roots, although appendages closely resembling these organs might be present, e.g., see *Caulerpa prolifera* and *Alaria esculenta*. The distinction is made on the basis of the presence or absence of conducting tissues, known technically as xylem and phloem. The xylem conducts water throughout the plant, and the phloem is involved in food translocation. The two tissues, always associated with each other within the plant, make up what is called the vascular system. Leaves, stems, and roots are vascularized. The appendages of algae, which look like leaves, stems, and roots, are without vascular tissue, although in some there are cells which bear a remarkable resemblance to the phloem cells of flowering plants.

In addition, the algae do not produce seeds as do flowering plants and gymnosperms. Instead, a variety of microscopic cells known as spores are produced, and these serve as the reproductive structures. The absence of seeds and the lack of vascular tissue, along with other features such as shape, appearance, size, and habitat, distinguish the algae as a distinct assemblage of plants.

Four major groups of macroscopic algae are found in marine habitats. They are known by the common names blue-green algae, green algae, brown algae, and red algae. Other groups of algae also occur, some in considerable abundance, such as diatoms and dinoflagellates, but they are microscopic organisms and therefore are not described in this manual. The blue-green algae, although common and conspicuous as slippery, slimy coverings on jetties, wharfs, intertidal rocks, and similar places, likewise are omitted, not because they are microscopic but because they are difficult to identify without magnification. To be sure, patches of blue-green algae can generally be recognized by their color and very slippery texture, but for identification a microscope is required. Let it suffice to point out here that the treacherous footing and hazardous walking on wet rocks and piers is usually due to the presence of these extremely slippery plants and they should be sidestepped at all times so as to avoid injury through falling.

The red, brown, and green algae, so named because each group exhibits a predominant color according to the abundance of specific pigments present within the plant, are given preferential treatment in this manual. They constitute the bulk of the seaweeds likely to be noticed on a walk along the beach. The identification of an alga by color alone is not totally reliable, but the pigments within a group are consistent to the extent that variations in color are attributable to such things as growing depth, bleaching, drying, and decay, rather than inherent differences. Thus, while all red algae are not red and all brown algae are not necessarily a deep chocolate brown, the color exhibited by a reasonably fresh "weed" will permit ready identification of the group to which it belongs. There will be exceptions, of course, but they will probably be rare, and as long as the user of this manual is cognizant of the existence of these exceptions he will not be disturbed if a particular seaweed seems to defy categorization.

How to Use This Manual

For convenience and quick identification the algae described in this book are grouped according to color. By turning to the proper color section the reader has immediately narrowed and simplified the identification of the plant in question.

Following the sections dealing with algae the two sea grasses (vascular plants) common to the Atlantic Coast are described. Commonly referred to as grasses, they are not members of the grass family, the Gramineae, but they are close relatives. Animals which might be mistaken for seaweeds are described next.

Each group of plants described is preceded by a brief description of the assemblage which in botanical terminology is known as a division. The derivation or meaning of the division name is given followed by comments about the group as a whole.

Within the division, each plant illustrated is described as to appearance, geographical distribution, size, and, where feasible, economic importance. Southernmost distributions are arbitrarily limited to the Florida Keys and Caribbean, although some of the species are known to occur as far south as Brazil. The descriptive terms used are nontechnical, insofar as possible, but where this was not possible a botanical term is used and is defined in the glossary at the end of the book. Such terms have been kept to a minimum.

The scientific (binomial) name of each plant will be found at the top of the page on the left-hand side. The name is composed of two parts, the generic name, always capitalized, and a specific epithet which is usually descriptive and not capitalized unless taken from the name of a person or another genus. For scientific precision and accuracy it is customary to give the name(s) of the author(s) after the scientific name. Frequently authors' names are abbreviated, a recommendation in the International Rules of Botanical Nomenclature. The abbreviations are established by usage, and those making use of them are ordinarily aware of the author's full name. A full listing of authors' names can be found in more technical floras and manuals.

In some instances an author's name is found in parentheses following the specific epithet. This indicates only that a taxonomic revision has taken place and will probably be of little interest to most users of this book. In those instances where only the generic name is given followed by an author's name, the plants are described at the generic level, either because of difficulties surrounding species identification without microscopic examination or because a number of species are presented and an introduction of the genus was thought desirable.

The common name or names, if there are any, are given on the top right-hand side of the page. It is likely that some common names used in specific locales will not be found. This in general is due to the lack of awareness that such names exist rather than an oversight. In any case, no attempt has been made to compile a complete list of common names.

The descriptive comments made for each plant, combined with known geographical ranges, type habitat, and illustration(s), should permit ready identification of the specimen in hand provided the user is in the proper color section of the book. It should be pointed out again, however, that only the most common of seaweeds, those most likely to be encountered, are included. The guide is not intended to be all-inclusive.

3

Using Seaweeds for Decorative Purposes

Throughout this guide, reference is made to the decorative uses of some of the plants described. On the assumption that some users of this book might wish to try their hand at making pictures, Christmas cards, place mats, or colorful stationery, a few comments on how it is done might be in order.

Only fresh seaweeds should be used, and these should be cleansed of undesirable epiphytes or parts before mounting. This can be achieved by floating the plant in a shallow pan of seawater and removing undesirable debris with a forceps or small brush.

The cleaned plant should then be refloated in a pan of water (a white enamel pan, shallow cake tin, or cafeteria tray serves the purpose nicely) and a sheet of herbarium paper (obtainable from any biological supply house), good grade typing paper, or nonglossy cardboard should be inserted under the plant and totally submerged. The paper must be thoroughly wet if water marks and unmanageable wrinkling of the paper when dried is to be avoided.

The plant is then carefully spread over the mounting paper in an artistic fashion according to the desires of the "artist" and the entire mount slowly lifted from the pan, the water being allowed to run off the edges of the sheet. A small brush or tweezers may be useful in spreading stubborn branches of fine delicate specimens. The sheet with specimen in place is then placed on blotting paper, likewise obtainable from a biological supply house, or on absorbent cardboard or even newspapers and a sheet of wax paper spread over the mounted plant. Another blotter or newspaper is placed over this, and additional specimens, prepared in a similar manner, placed on top of the first. The mounted and stacked specimens are then dried using either a plant press or heavy books to press the plants while they are drying. Heat should not be applied, although placing the mounted specimens in a warm room or in the sun will speed the drying and do no harm. Changing the newspapers or blotters once or twice will also help speed the process.

The plants, in most instances, will adhere to the mounting paper by means of their own mucilage. Tough wiry specimens or calcified plants may have to be glued to the paper but no rule of thumb applies here; each specimen has to be treated separately depending upon intended use. After several days the specimens should be dry and can be removed from the press, trimmed to desired size, and used accordingly. If kept out of strong light they will retain their natural color for many years. I have, for example, in my library a collection of algae in book form which were collected and mounted in 1833 by a resident of Newport, Rhode Island. They still have their natural color and could, if one were willing to take the time, be identified as to species. On my desk I have two plastic coasters with colorful algae pressed and arranged decoratively within. They were sent to me by Dr. Richard Lee, a friend at Scripps Institution of Oceanography in California. Not long ago I received a letter from Australia with small pieces of red algae permanently pressed to the stationery in an artistic fashion, and the walls of the Phycological Herbarium next to my office are graced by pictures made from herbarium mounts. One year I surprised the students in my phycology course by sending each of them a Christmas card made from a carefully mounted feathery seaweed. Thus, the uses of preserved marine plants above and beyond the scientific are limited only by one's imagination.

The Green Algae

Division *Chlorophycophyta*

Gr. *chlorōs*, green + *phykos*,
seaweed + *phyton*, plant

The algae in this division are a grassy green color due to a predominance of the green pigment chlorophyll, the pigment found in all photosynthetic plants. In both the brown and red algae the chlorophyll is masked by the presence of other pigments; nevertheless, they too are photosynthetic.

Over 7,000 species of green algae have been described of which about 13% are marine. Members of the division range in size from microscopic plants (visible only with a microscope) to individual plants 15 or more inches in length. The diversity in form and size, particularly in the warm-water genera, makes this group of algae one of the more attractive and interesting of all marine flora.

Many of the species cannot properly be identified without the use of microscopic characteristics, but in the main the genera most likely to be encountered by the casual beach visitor can be identified rather easily on the basis of size, shape, and locality.

All green algae are economically important because of the part they play in the biological food chain, a sequence of predator-prey events which ultimately affect and involve man. But some species of *Chlorophycophyta* are of particular significance because they are consumed directly by man, either in salads or as marine vegetables. Others have been the subjects of intensive investigations in the research laboratory, contributing greatly to man's knowledge of basic biological processes. Their simplicity of structure makes them ideal for this purpose.

So common are green algae along the Atlantic coast that it would be a rare day indeed should the shore visitor fail to see some member of the group. The ubiquitous "sea lettuce" is the most likely to be found, but there are others equally common. All are attractive in their own special way.

Enteromorpha intestinalis (L.) Link   Link Confetti

A dozen or more species of *Enteromorpha* are to be found along the Atlantic coast, and variability within species, as well as certain resemblances to species of *Cladophora*, makes positive identification difficult. However, *E. intestinalis* is common enough along the east coast to warrant its inclusion here as representative of the genus, even though the chances of other species of *Enteromorpha* being mistaken for it are good.

Commonly found in tide pools and somewhat protected areas, this alga is generally recognized by its bright green to yellow-green color and its tubular, intestinal appearance. The plant body may reach a diameter of 1 to 2 inches and a length of more than a yard, although specimens less than 1 foot in length are more frequently encountered. Thalli may occur singly or in clumps, attached to rocks, shells, and wharfs. The tubular, saclike blade of the plant, with numerous constrictions, is gas-filled. This feature accounts for the specific epithet. When submerged, the inflated blades, which are attached to the substrate by threadlike outgrowths from the base of the plant, spread gracefully in the water. Out of water the blades become flattened and matted.

Almost worldwide in distribution and found in brackish as well as pure sea water, *E. intestinalis* is common along the Atlantic coast from the Gulf of St. Lawrence to Florida. It is quite tolerant of salinity changes and may grow on the hulls of ships traveling between sea and river ports. Most characteristically it grows just below low tide and may be found the year around.

Link confetti, along with other species of *Enteromorpha*, is a basic food for fishes, crabs, and other marine animals. It reportedly is consumed as a vegetable in some parts of Hawaii, China, and the Philippine Islands.

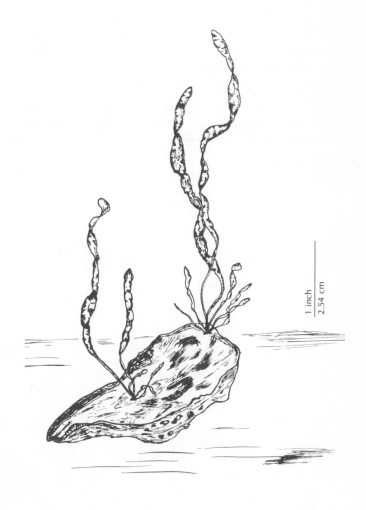

1 inch
2.54 cm

Enteromorpha intestinalis—attached to an oyster shell, showing the inflated intestinal appearance of the thallus.

Monostroma oxyspermum (Kützing) Doty

Resembling sheets of wet, green tissue paper, *M. oxyspermum* is an alga which can be found in shallow water from Newfoundland to the Florida Keys. Plants may be attached singly or in tufts to stones, shells, marine grasses, and other submerged objects or may be found detached and free-floating in quiet pools where individual blades often reach a length of 2 feet. The alga is frequently found in brackish water, especially salt-marsh inlets and drainage ditches. In Florida it is often found attached to mangrove roots.

Light green to chartreuse in color, this seaweed is delicate in appearance even when submerged, and when handled the blades tear quite easily. The membranous plant body is only one cell thick and somewhat gelatinous in texture. In New England the alga is rather uncommon in summer, but it may be found the year around along the Florida coast. It is a regular part of the diet for many marine animals. In Japan, certain species of *Monostroma* are cultivated along with the red alga *Porphyra* for the manufacture of Nori, a popular food in the Orient.

Monostroma oxyspermum—with blades expanded, as it appears submerged.

1 inch
2.54 cm

Ulva lactuca L.   Sea Lettuce

The common name given to this alga is most descriptive, for the dark green plant body, attached by a rhizoidal holdfast to submerged rocks, shells, pilings, or other seaweeds, is frequently composed of a number of blades which resemble a loosely arranged head of leaf lettuce. Although normally attached, *Ulva* often occurs in free-floating masses on the bottoms of shallow pools and brackish ponds. Drifting fragments and dried remnants of plants can usually be found along any beach from Florida to Newfoundland. The alga is probably the most commonly encountered of all seaweeds.

The blades of *Ulva* are membranous, relatively broad, and may be 20 or more inches in length. They are more substantial than the blades of the closely related genus *Monostroma*, being two cells thick rather than one. When growing in abundance, beds of *Ulva* may hamper the movements of waders and foul the lines and nets of fishermen. However, the plants provide shelter for numerous marine animals and undoubtedly serve as food for others. When dry the blades are blackened and brittle.

In the Orient *U. lactuca* is used in salads and as a garnishment. In some regions it is used as food for hogs and other domestic animals, and several species are used for medicinal purposes.

1 inch
2.54 cm

Ulva lactuca—showing membranous lettucelike blades.

Chaetomorpha linum (Müller) Kützing

Conspicuous only when occurring en masse, this bright green to yellowish green alga might be compared in appearance to raveled thread from a knitted green sweater. The plant body is filamentous, unattached, and somewhat stiff and crinkled. Upon close inspection the filaments appear jointed or articulated with dark green bands. This feature allows for quick and easy identification.

Plants may be found the year around from the shores of Nova Scotia south to Florida. They probably serve as food for a number of marine animals, although the stiff, somewhat coarse texture of the alga may discourage such use. The tangled colonies provide easily accessible protective shelter for small fishes and other marine organisms.

In the South Pacific some species of Chaetomorpha are eaten in salads by the natives.

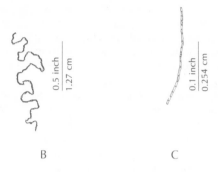

B   C

A

Chaetomorpha linum—(A) tangled masses growing in eelgrass bed; (B) filament enlarged showing the typical crinkled appearance of thallus; (C) cellular nature of a filament as seen with 10X magnification.

Cladophora Kützing

There are many species of this seaweed along our Atlantic coast, but only an expert with the aid of a microscope can properly identify them. The plants are of such common occurrence that even the casual beachcomber is likely to see one or more species floating in tide pools, matted on coastal rocks, or growing in patches on mud flats between tide levels. Submerged stones, sea shells, coral fragments, jetties, wharfs, and boat bottoms are all likely places for growth of these seaweeds. A resemblance to certain species of *Enteromorpha* is strong.

The plants are filamentous and hairlike, growing in tufts, mats, or in loose floating masses which resemble wet, green hair, if that can be imagined. The color of the plants varies from bright green to yellow-green, gray-green, or olive-green. The texture also varies from smooth and velvety to stiff and somewhat coarse. Attachment to the substrate is by means of branched, threadlike outgrowths from basal cells. Masses of these algae can easily be torn from their holdfasts. In this manner many of the floating colonies originate. The individual filaments are sparingly to repeatedly branched so colonies are usually quite entangled.

The genus is widespread from Newfoundland to Florida with many freshwater species in addition to the marine species. As might be expected, the plants are frequent inhabitants of brackish water and in all localities most likely serve as food for fish and other animals. Clumps of these plants may clog drainage screens, overgrow wires, or completely cover the bottom of shallow ponds or the walls of aquatic enclosures. Consequently the alga is often viewed as nothing but a nuisance. In Hawaii, however, one local species is eaten with freshwater shrimp and salt.

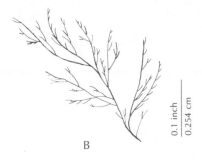

B

0.1 inch
0.254 cm

A

3 inches
7.62 cm

Cladophora species—(A) habit sketch showing attachment of thallus to a rock; (B) enlargement of plant body showing the characteristic branching of a filament.

Spongomorpha Kützing

Four species of this alga are known to occur from New Jersey north to Baffin Island. The species are separated on the basis of microscopic characteristics.

The plants are filamentous, bright green to dark green, and grow in tufts on various objects, including larger algae, in tide pools and on exposed rocky shores.

The filaments are attached by rhizoidal branches from the lower cells. Individual plants may reach a length of 6 inches but in general are smaller than are the filaments of *Cladophora*, the seaweed which they most closely resemble.

The distribution of *Spongomorpha* is more limited than *Cladophora*, restricted to temperate and boreal coastlines. Like *Cladophora*, the filaments of *Spongomorpha* are probably grazed by many marine animals.

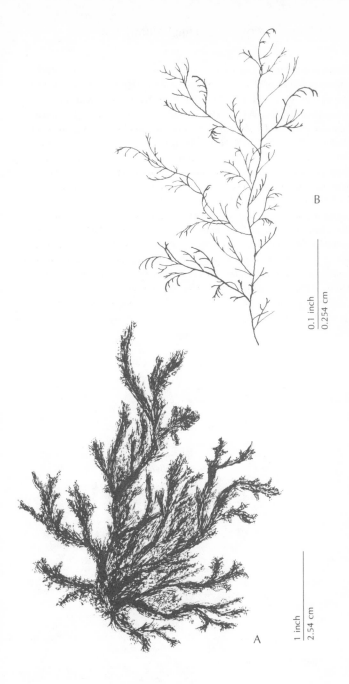

Spongomorpha species—(A) habit sketch showing matted appearance of a tuft; (B) enlargement of a filament showing incurved branch tips and mode of branching.

Avrainvillea longicaulis (Kützing) Murray & Boodle

Found only along the southern coasts of the United States, the velvety, rather thick, spongy blade and the cylindrical to slightly compressed stipe to which the blade is attached give this seaweed an overall appearance of a dull green spatula stuck in the sand, handle end down. Individual plants may reach a height of 8 inches and may be found singly or growing in clusters with several blades arising from a massive holdfast of entwined rhizoids. The alga is usually found growing in the sand and mud of somewhat protected beaches, frequently in quiet waters under or between fishing piers and boat docks. Its range is reported to be from North Carolina south into tropical waters.

Like so many of the warm-water green algae, the form of *Avrainvillea* is so bizarre that there are few other marine plants with which it might be confused. The group of plants to which it belongs, the Siphonales, is itself unique for all members of the order are coenocytic, i.e., the plant body is multinucleate and nonseptate. When in combination with other tropical marine algae such as species of *Penicillus*, the shaving-brush alga, and *Caulerpa*, *Avrainvillea* contributes to a rather spectacular and unique appearing submerged flora.

0.5 inch
1.27 cm

Avrainvillea longicaulis—habit sketch showing spatulate, spongy blades and cylindrical to slightly compressed stipes.

Bryopsis plumosa (Hudson) C. Agardh

A coenocytic alga of tide pools and sheltered places, *B. plumosa* grows in bushy tufts resembling miniature ferns or clusters of light to olive green feathers. Resemblance to the latter accounts for the specific name given this plant.

The alga reportedly may be found all along the Atlantic coast, from Nova Scotia to Florida, but a preference is shown to the warmer waters from Cope Cod southward.

Each blade of the plant consists of a central axis with many branchlets. Decreasing size of the branchlets from the base of the blade to.the apex gives each blade a pyramidal shape. The branchlets are pinnately arranged with the lower portion of the blade axis generally naked. The tufts are attached to the substratum by rhizoids. The alga probably is grazed for food by a variety of marine invertebrates.

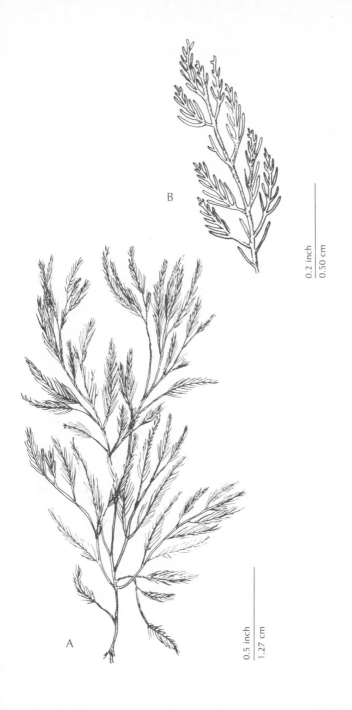

B

0.2 inch
0.50 cm

0.5 inch
1.27 cm

A

Bryopsis plumosa—(A) whole plant; (B) magnified view of branch tip.

Caulerpa Lamouroux

Unique among the green algae because of the odd, beautiful form, species of *Caulerpa* are generally easy to recognize. The plant body is differentiated into a rhizoidal, a stoloniferous, and an erect portion, the latter yellow-green to dark green and quite variable in appearance. The plants are coenocytic, i.e., nonseptate, branched, and often wide spreading. Just below the low-tide level, in shallow waters, extensive colonies of *Caulerpa* may be found growing attached in sand or on rocks, coral fragments, shells, and sometimes mangrove roots.

Identification of species is chiefly on the basis of the appearance of the erect branches and, although there is much ecotypic variation, recognition of the more common species is not difficult.

Little is known of the extent to which *Caulerpa* is used as food by marine animals, but there can be little doubt of the useful role these plants play in providing protective shelter for numerous invertebrates and small fishes.

The species are strictly warm-water plants, distributed from North Carolina south into the tropics.

Caulerpa mexicana (Sonder) J. Agardh

Fairly common in lagoons and shallow inlets where it grows attached to small stones and shells on sandy or muddy bottoms, *C. mexicana* may reach a length of 10 to 12 inches, but the species is quite variable and in some areas may be dwarfed. The foliar branches are pinnately divided into flat, oval·to oblong pinnae up to ½ inch in length. The pinnae are arranged oppositely on a flat and somewhat broad midrib. The flatness of the foliar branches, which may reach a height of 10 inches, is distinctive.

The slender, branching stolons bear descending rhizoidal branches at short intervals, generally between the upright branches.

Plants are a light green to yellow-green color, the foliar branches smooth and glossy.

The species is not known to occur north of Florida. It may be found growing in very shallow as well as very deep waters, having been dredged from a depth of 225 feet.

1 inch
—————
2.54 cm

Caulerpa mexicana—habit sketch of plant showing the flat, pinnately divided, foliar branches, the creeping stolon, and descending rhizoid-bearing branches.

Caulerpa paspaloides (Bory) Greville

Dark green in color and characterized by bushy branches arising from thick, strong stolons, *C. paspaloides* when submerged and free of epiphytes is a very attractive plant. It typically grows attached to rocks in shallow water along the Florida coast.

The stolon, up to ⅜ of an inch in diameter, produces upright axes with pronounced naked stipes bearing at their apex one to four foliar branches which in turn are subdivided into pinnately arranged branchlets densely covered with pinnae. Stipe and foliar branch combined may exceed 6 inches. Length of plants is frequently more than 15 inches.

Rhizoids, borne terminally on stout descending branches, occur at intervals along the stolon between the erect foliar axes.

The species has been reported from Florida south into the tropics. Several varieties and forms have been described on the basis of differences in the foliar branches and branchlets. In general, size and bushy appearance make the species readily identifiable.

2 inches
5.08 cm

Caulerpa paspaloides—the bushy, erect, foliar branches which arise from a thick, stout stolon characterize this species.

Caulerpa prolifera (Forsskål) Lamouroux

The erect, bright green, spatula-shaped branches of C. *prolifera* make this species easy to identify in the field. The sometimes large, wide-spreading colonies grow on sandy or muddy bottoms in shallow water with the slender stolons often covered by sand and only the stalked, erect, flat green branches visible. These may reach a height of 6 inches and a blade width of ½ inch.

The branched stolons bearing numerous, short, descending, rhizoid-tipped branches firmly attach the plants to the shifting substrate. Individual stolons are often more than a foot in length.

While the species is characteristically a shallow-water plant growing just below low-tide level, it has been dredged from great depths. The geographical range extends from North Carolina south into the Caribbean.

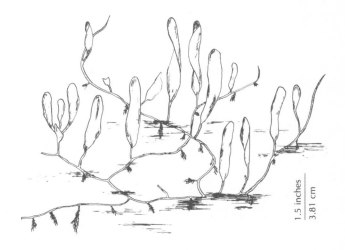

1.5 inches
3.81 cm

Caulerpa prolifera—colonies of this species are readily recognized by the spatula-shaped, erect branches. Stolons may be entirely or partially buried in the sand or mud.

Caulerpa sertularioides (Gmeln.) Howe

Flat, featherlike, erect branches, which may reach a height of 6 inches and a width of nearly ¾ inch, give *C. sertularioides* a very graceful appearance in the water. The upright branches are dark green to olive green in appearance and arise from coarse, moderately thick, branching stolons. The plants form large colonies in sandy areas. The feathery appearance is distinctive and quickly distinguishes the species from *C. mexicana*, which has broader, less flexible pinnae.

Rhizoids are produced at the tips of long, descending, sometimes forked branches which penetrate the sand to several inches, thus anchoring the plants firmly.

The species is typically found in shallow water but has been dredged from waters up to 300 feet deep. It is geographically distributed from Florida south into the tropics.

Caulerpa sertularioides is an important food of the natives of some Philippine Islands.

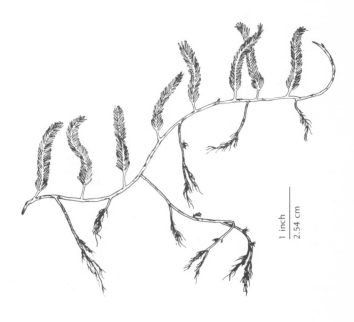

1 inch
2.54 cm

Caulerpa sertularioides—portion of thallus showing the feathery upright branches and long, rhizoid-bearing descending branches.

Codium Stackhouse

Because of their spongy texture, dichotomous branching, and deep green coloration, species of *Codium* are easily distinguished from other seaweeds. In fact, their bizarre appearance might lead the unwary to an identification of "some kind of sponge" rather than a green alga. But the coenocytic, filamentous construction of the thallus is evident upon close inspection.

There are six species of *Codium* to be found along the Atlantic coast. Five are warm-water plants distributed from the Carolinas southward. The sixth is a cold-water alga which has only recently become a part of the east coast seaweed flora. The species are separated chiefly on the basis of microscopic characteristics; macroscopically the plants appear much alike.

To aid the user of this guide in recognizing members of the genus, two species of *Codium* are described, the cold-water species and for comparison one of the warm-water plants. Although the two are similar in appearance they are not likely to be confused with each other due to their different geographical ranges.

Codium fragile (Suringar) Hariot	Oyster Thief, Sputnik Weed, Sea Staghorn, Dead Man's Fingers, Spaghetti Grass

Dark green in color, spongy in texture, and tubular in appearance, *C. fragile* is a newcomer to the northeast coast of North America. It was first reported in 1957 from East Marion, Long Island, New York, by two collectors of marine fauna. Since then it has spread both north and south and is now common along the shores of a number of states. Its abundance in some areas has seriously threatened the oyster beds, the shellfish often becoming completely covered with heavy growths of the alga. Larger plants tend to accumulate oxygen interstitially and eventually become so buoyant they pull the oysters to which they are attached from the oyster bed whence they are carried away by the currents. Thus the name "oyster thief." The species is believed to have spread from Japan.

Codium fragile is a cold-water alga which resembles in appearance *C. isthmocladum* Vickers and to some extent *C. decortatum* Howe, both common from North Carolina south. It has become quite abundant along the coast of Rhode Island and may be found in quantity as drift on some beaches.

The plant body is coenocytic (nonseptate) and dichotomously branched, the branches often more than ¼ inch in diameter. Individual plants may be more than 15 inches in height with numerous branches arising from a rhizoidal holdfast. A cross section of one of the branches, if

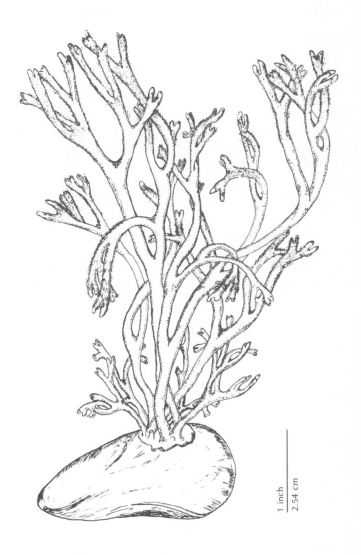

1 inch
2.54 cm

Codium fragile—habit sketch of a plant attached to a mussel.

slightly magnified, reveals a construction of intertwined filaments with inflated, sharply pointed, bulbous tips (utricles).

The geographical distribution along the Atlantic coast has not been precisely determined, but collections have been described from Assateaque Channel, Virginia, to Maine. Were it not for the threat to oyster beds, *C. fragile* might be considered an attractive addition to our seaweed flora. In Japan the plants are consumed as food, and related species are used similarly in Hawaii, Malaya, and the Philippine Islands.

Codium isthmocladum Vickers

One of several species of *Codium* found in the warm waters off the coast of the southeastern United States, *C. isthmocladum* is found in shallow water below low-tide levels and is also frequently found in the nets of shrimp fishermen. Like other species of *Codium* inhabiting warmer seas it is generally identified by the specialist on the basis of microscopic characters.

Codium isthmocladum grows erect, up to 8 inches tall, forming a bushy, dichotomously branched, light to dark green plant body. The branches are cylindrical and range in diameter from ⅛ inch to nearly ½ inch. A rhizoidal holdfast anchors the plant to the substratum.

The species is geographically distributed from North Carolina south into the Caribbean. There is a close resemblance to *C. fragile*, but the plants do not reach the size of the latter species and the geographical ranges do not overlap. Thus it is not likely the two species will be confused.

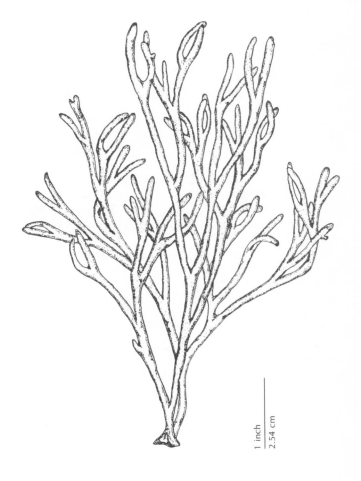

1 inch
2.54 cm

Codium isthmocladum—habit sketch of plant.

Halimeda Lamouroux

At least seven species of the coenocytic genus *Halimeda* are known to occur along the Florida coast. Of these, several are so common in shallow water near the low-tide line as to be seen by even the casual observer.

The plant body is quite distinct, being divided into calcified segments with flexible connecting joints. The plants grow erect, up to 12 or more inches in height, from rhizoidal holdfasts which may become massive. Branching is frequently profuse, the light green to whitish green color of the branches aiding in quick identification of the genus. The basic structure of the plants is filamentous, but this is detectable only through microscopic examination of sections of the thallus.

The calcification of the plants makes it unlikely that they would be grazed to any extent by marine animals. However, large colonies spreading over sandy, gravelly, and sometimes rocky areas are not uncommon, and these offer convenient shelter to small fishes and invertebrates.

Halimeda incrassata (Ellis) Lamouroux

Arising from a single, frequently massive holdfast of rhizoids, *H. incrassata* reaches a height of 8 to 10 inches and is of common occurrence in sandy areas where it frequently grows among sea "grasses" and other algae. Branching is lavish from a robust, sometimes forked stalk which is heavily calcified and often covered with epiphytes.

Distal segments of free branches are oval to triangular in shape, flat, and light green to olive green. Basal segments may be cylindrical or slightly compressed and are generally pale green to greenish white. The broad, flat segments, arranged end to end into broadening fan-shaped branches, are distinctive. Two forms are separated within the species on the basis of segment differences.

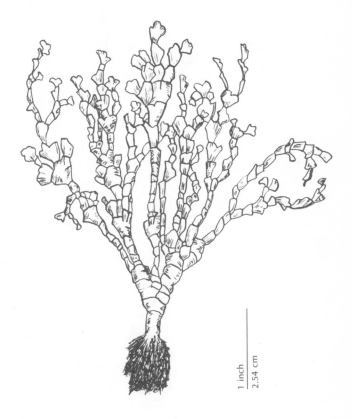

1 inch
2.54 cm

Halimeda incrassata—a single plant showing the massive rhizoidal holdfast and the triangular segments of the photosynthetic branches.

Halimeda monile (Ellis & Solander) Lamouroux

Segments of the plant body are predominantly cylindrical in this species, up to ¼ inch long and mostly less than ⅛ inch in diameter. The plants are dark green, noticeably calcified, and bushy. Branching is from a short stalk attached to the substratum by a bulbous rhizoidal holdfast. Individual plants may reach a height of 9 or 10 inches.

The species is found in shallow water near the low-tide level. Two forms within the species are generally recognized, separated on the basis of the extent of branching and appearance of segments.

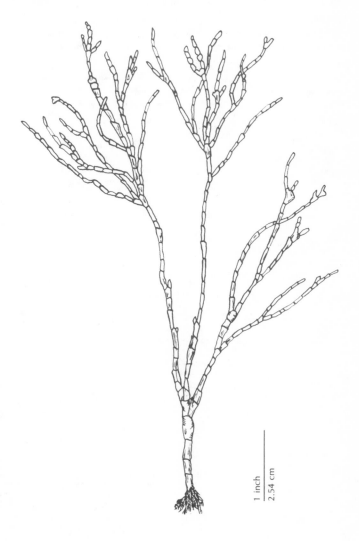

1 inch / 2.54 cm

Halimeda monile—the elongated, cylindrical segments of the branches in this species are distinctive.

Halimeda opuntia (L.) Lamouroux

More than one fisherman has probably fouled his line in growths of *H. opuntia*, for the species typically grows in large clumps on sand, gravel, and rocks in shallow waters not exposed to strong wave action. The wide-spreading, lateral growth of the plant from an original rhizoidal holdfast, but with many places of attachment as the plant increases in size, is distinctive and separates the species from all others.

Halimeda opuntia may reach a height of 10 inches, but lateral growth far exceeds growth in height so that large clusters of the plant are common. Colonies are a pale green to whitish green color due to heavy calcification. Branching is random in all directions, the individual segments often at right angles to each other, flattened, trilobed, and up to ¾ inch broad and ½ inch long. Within the species three forms are recognized on the basis of segment shape and colony size.

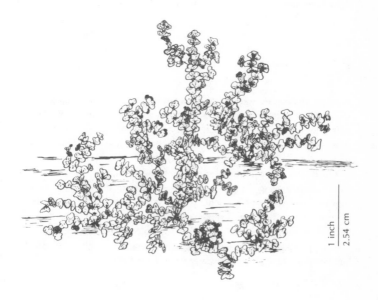

1 inch
2.54 cm

Halimeda opuntia—habit sketch of plant showing the wide-spreading growth form and the flattened, trilobed segments of the thallus.

Penicillus Lamarck   Shaving Brush Alga

The common name given to species of *Penicillus* is most appropriate, for individual plants do indeed look like shaving brushes. Individuals grow erect, up to 6 inches tall, with a tuft of dichotomously branched filaments arising from a simple, robust stalk anchored to the substratum by rhizoids. All are coenocytic.

The thalli are lightly calcified so that individual plants have a whitish green color except for the extreme tips of the filaments, which may be a bright green.

Four species have been reported as occurring along the Florida coast southward into the Caribbean. They are for the most part plants of sandy, protected shallow bays where they intermingle with species of *Caulerpa, Halimeda, Udotea*, and sea "grasses," forming bizarre plant communities.

It is unlikely that these plants are of much value to animal life other than as hosts for sedentary species. They perhaps serve as minor food sources to a few invertebrates. They are in no way related to the fungus *Penicillium* from which the antibiotic penicillin is obtained.

Penicillus capitatus Lamarck

A very common and somewhat characteristic plant of shallow bays and lagoons, *P. capitatus* is generally easy to recognize because of its long stalk and its oblong to spherical "brush" of filaments. The plants are substantially calcified, the stalks up to 4 inches in length. The filamentous tufts are little more than 1 to 1½ inches in length.

The individual filaments are very slender, but because of the calcification they are rather tough. Slight magnification reveals their repeated dichotomous branching. The stalks appear spongy under magnification. They are slightly constricted at their base where the bulbous mass of rhizoids arises. Color of the plants is light green.

Two forms of the species are recognized, using the length of the stalk and length of the filaments as segregating characteristics.

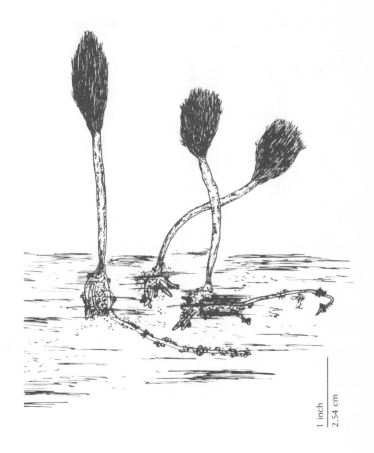

1 inch
2.54 cm

Penicillus capitatus—habit sketch of three plants showing the characteristic long stalks and filamentous tufts.

Penicillus dumentosus (Lamouroux) Blainville

Conspicuous in shallow waters because of its large size (individual plants may reach a height of 6 inches) and slightly tapered, somewhat flattened stalk, *P. dumentosus* is a common species along the Florida coast. Plants may occur in considerable numbers in the quiet waters of protected inlets and shallow waters under docks and along jetties.

The stalks of this species range from 1 to 3 inches in length and are somewhat fan-shaped as they broaden from the rhizoidal base to the apex. The lightly calcified bright green filaments form large tufts often 3 or more inches in length and rather wide-spreading. Individual filaments branch dichotomously at their tips, and although soft in texture, they are relatively strong and do not readily break.

A bulbous mass of rhizoids, often with loose, somewhat stringy, ropelike strands extending laterally, anchors the plant in the sand.

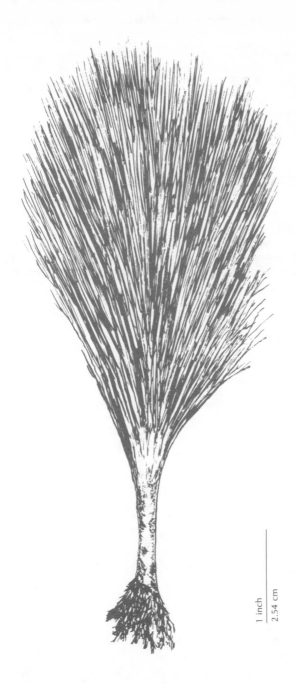

1 inch
—
2.54 cm

Penicillus dumentosus—the common name "shaving brush alga"
is especially appropriate for this species.

Rhipocephalus phoenix (Ellis & Solander) Kützing

Tufted and stalked, erect and calcified, *R. phoenix* superficially resembles the genus *Penicillus*, but the branching filaments of the tuft form small, overlapping fan-shaped blades which give the plant a cropped or closely trimmed appearance. Slight magnification of the blade reveals the filamentous structure.

Growing in shallow waters in sandy areas, this bizarre coenocytic alga is frequently found intermingled with species of *Penicillus, Halimeda,* and *Caulerpa*, but its appearance is so strikingly different, because of the cuneate blades, that it is easily identified.

Individual plants may be 3 to 4 inches tall, the tuft cone-shaped and dull olive green in color. The stalks are smooth and highly calcified, whitish to tan colored, and cylindrical in shape. A basal, closely intermingled mass of rhizoids attaches the plant to the substratum.

Strictly tropical in habit, *R. phoenix* may be found along the southern Florida coast and southward into the Caribbean. It is unlikely that the plants are eaten by marine animals because of the calcification, but little is known about this.

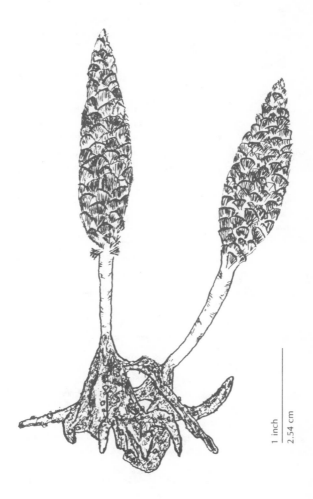

1 inch

2.54 cm

Rhipocephalus phoenix—two plants showing the fan-shaped overlapping blades and intermingled mass of rhizoids.

Udotea Lamouroux

Plants belonging to this genus have funnel-shaped or fanlike blades, the latter the more frequent, so the common name given to these algae is both descriptive and appropriate.

Growing erect and reaching a height of 8 or more inches, each plant consists of a blade which terminates a simple, occasionally branched, cylindrical to slightly flattened stalk anchored to the substratum by a tangled mass of rhizoids.

The thalli are lightly to substantially calcified with the color varying from gray-green to olive green. Structurally, the blade and stalk are composed of branched coenocytic filaments, but this is not detectable without magnification.

Eight species have been described, geographically distributed from the North Carolina coast south to Florida and on into the Caribbean. Some species are characteristically deep-water plants, but several are common in shallow water where they intermingle with other equally bizarre marine algae. Little is known of the extent to which *Udotea* species serve as food for marine animals, but where abundant the plants undoubtedly provide shelter for small fishes and invertebrates. Smaller algae colonize the blades and stalks.

Udotea flabellum (Ellis & Solander) Lamouroux

The blades of this species are broadly fan-shaped and conspicuously banded by alternating dark and light zones which simulate annual rings or growth increments. Structurally, the darker bands are areas where corticating filaments are especially well developed and cover the central axial filaments. The lighter bands are areas where the covering is not so complete.

Individual plants often reach a height of 6 to 8 inches with a blade that is quite flexible despite heavy calcification. Stalks are from 1 to 1½ inches long, flattened near the blade and irregularly cylindrical near the dense basal mass of rhizoids.

Color varies from gray-green to dark olive green with touches of brown. The species is common in shallow waters along the Florida coast, frequently intermingled with sea "grasses" in sandy areas.

1 inch
2.54 cm

Udotea flabellum—habit sketch showing the broad, fan-shaped blade and the distinctive bands of corticating filaments.

Udotea spinulosa Howe

Whitish in color and velvety to spongy in appearance, this species of *Udotea* does not have the readily visible bands of alternating dark and light zones so characteristic of *U. flabellum*. Close inspection of the fan-shaped blade reveals some banding, but it is barely distinguishable.

Udotea spinulosa is seldom more than 3 inches tall. The stalks are cylindrical to slightly flattened where attached to the blade, smooth or spongy in appearance and rather short, less than 1 inch in length. The basal holdfast is small and inconspicuous, composed of numerous rhizoids.

The species occurs in both shallow and deep waters, especially in sandy areas. Individual plants may escape notice because of their small size and whitish coloring, but occasionally extensive colonies are found in the sandy shallows of rocky ledges.

0.5 inch
1.27 cm

Udotea spinulosa—three plants showing the flat, fan-shaped blades and the absence of distinct bands of corticating filaments compared with *U. flabellum*.

Acetabularia crenulata   Mermaid's Wineglass
Lamouroux

Mermaid's wineglass is certainly an appropriate name for this tropical alga because individual plants resemble, with a little imagination, delicate frosted wine glasses with long stalks. The stalks, up to 3 inches long, bear at their summit one or more whorls of branchlets which form tiny cups or slightly flattened funnel-shaped discs. Minute branched hairs occur on the upper surface of the disc.

Both stalks and discs are lime encrusted, giving the alga a whitish green color and sufficient rigidity to stand upright in the water. Without the calcification these delicate algae would certainly be prostrate and less attractive.

Close inspection of the discs reveals the lateral association of the branchlets and reflects the filamentous construction of the thallus. The plants are anchored to the substratum by lobed rhizoidal holdfasts.

Commonly occurring in dense colonies in the shallow waters of protected lagoons and mangrove swamps, *A. crenulata* grows on shells, stones, limestone ledges, and mangrove roots. Its geographical range extends southward from Florida. It is of little economic significance, although, because of its structure, it has been used extensively in research laboratories for the study of growth processes.

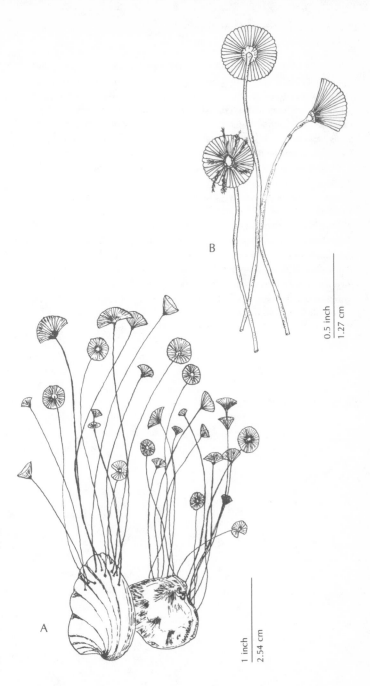

Acetabularia crenulata—(A) habit sketch of colonies attached to sea shells; (B) enlargement of distal portions of stalks showing radial symmetry of discs, upper and lower surface.

Batophora oerstedi J. Agardh

Usually found growing in clusters in quiet waters of lagoons or mangrove thickets, this alga is, en masse, unattractive and generally inconspicuous. If slightly magnified, however, individual plants are seen to consist of a long, thin, cylindrical-shaped, axial cell bearing many whorls of forked branches. The symmetry and beauty of the alga can then be readily appreciated, for each plant superficially resembles a miniature bottle brush or, if fruiting, an elongated cluster of grapes or a tiny grape hyacinth plant.

Bright green to olive green and anywhere from 1 to 4 inches in height, the alga is not calcified and is therefore delicate. Nevertheless, the plants grow erect although usually in rather dense clusters. The axial cells are attached by branched rhizoidal holdfasts.

Batophora oerstedi is distributed from Florida southward and is reported to be tolerant of brackish to freshwater habitats. Little is known of the extent to which the plants might be grazed by marine animals, but due to the lack of calcification they may indeed be eaten by a variety of invertebrates and small fish. One variety, occidentalis (Harvey) Howe, is recognized as being a small plant seldom over 1½ inches in height with closely set whorls of branches.

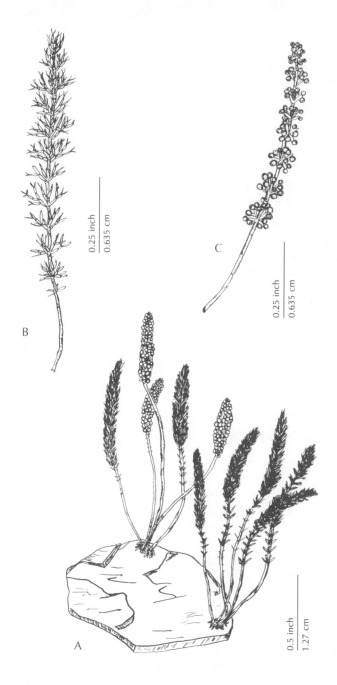

Batophora oerstedi—(A) habitat sketch of colonies growing on a stone; (B) magnified view of vegetative plant showing whorls of forked branches; (C) fruiting plant.

Cladophoropsis membranacea (C. Agardh) Børgensen

Frequently found growing in large clumps or tuftlike mounds, C. membranacea might easily be mistaken for an aquatic moss for in gross form it superficially resembles a clump of the pin-cushion moss, Leucobryum glaucum (Hedw.) Ångstr. ex Fr., so common to north temperate hardwood forests. The resemblance is accentuated by the color of the alga, which is normally a very light green but turning whitish as the plants dry. Leucobryum likewise is a light green color when wet but whitish when inadequately moistened.

The thallus is filamentous and much branched, forming an entangled mass of erect or semierect filaments arising from multicellular holdfasts. The distinctive characteristic of the alga is the absence of cross walls at the bases of the branches, but this feature is visible only under high magnification.

The alga is found along the coast of Georgia and Florida and the islands of the Caribbean. It typically grows on stones and ledges in the intertidal zone, sometimes forming large thick mats. In all likelihood small marine fauna feed on the plants since they are fine textured, but little is known about this. At low tide, clumps of this alga could adequately protect any number of small invertebrates from desiccation.

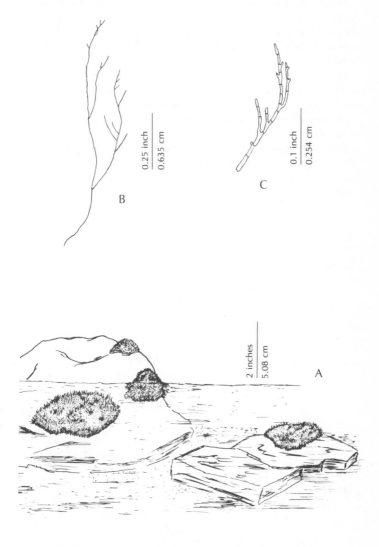

Cladophoropsis membranacea—(A) typical habitat of the alga showing appearance out of water and submerged; (B) enlargement of a filament showing mode of branching; (C) cellular detail of filament.

Dasycladus vermicularis (Scopoli) Krasser

This green alga is similar to *Batophora oerstedi* in structure, being composed of an elongated axial cell bearing numerous whorls of forked branchlets. The whorls are closer together, however, giving the alga a spongy rather than brushlike appearance.

The individual plants are small, 1 to 2 inches in height, up to ¼ inch in diameter, and an olive green color. They usually grow in clumps from rhizoidal holdfasts. The close-set whorls, spongy texture, and elongate cylindrical form account for the specific epithet *vermicularis*, meaning wormlike.

Occurring along the coast of Florida and the islands of the Caribbean, *D. vermicularis* is a shallow-water alga growing in rather exposed places and sometimes almost covering shells and sand-covered stones. Sand particles are frequently embedded between the branches making the visual observation of branch whorls difficult.

Being without calcification, like *Bathophora*, it is quite likely that this alga is a source of food for many small fishes and invertebrates.

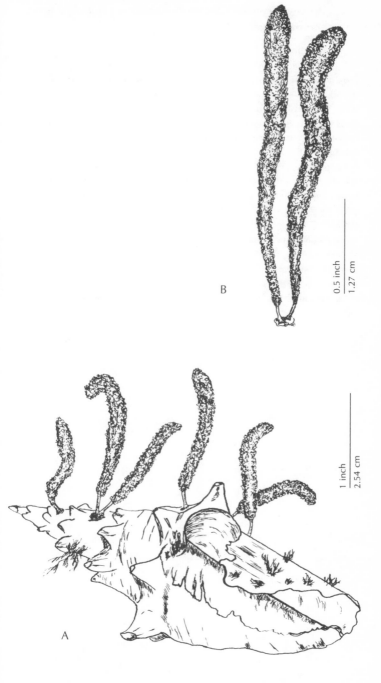

Dasycladus vermicularis—(A) habit sketch; (B) two plants enlarged showing holdfasts and spongy texture of thallus.

Dictyosphaeria cavernosa (Forsskål) Børgesen

Green Bubble Alga

This spherical to irregularly shaped alga is easily recognized by its warty surface, which with slight magnification appears honeycombed. The spheres, usually hollow, may be partially collapsed and saucer-shaped. When several plants are associated with each other and flattened, as they frequently are in drift specimens, the overall appearance is one of thick, "potato chip" layers of green plant material stuck together. Colony diameters may be 4 or more inches.

The plants are multicellular and attached to the substratum by rhizoids. The vegetative cells are large and angular or polygonal in shape, thus explaining the "warty" surface appearance. A light green to olive green color, these cells form a single-layered, solid thallus wall which is fairly stiff and rigid.

Dictyosphaeria cavernosa is frequently encountered on sandy beaches as drift material. The plants typically grow attached to rocks in the intertidal zone but have been dredged from depths of over 150 feet. The species is found along the coast of Florida.

No information is available as to the plants' usefulness as food for marine fauna, but drift material may be eaten by hermit crabs and other scavengers of the beach.

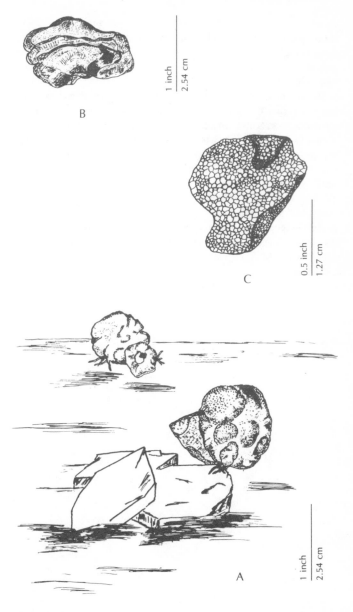

Dictyosphaeria cavernosa—(A) habit sketch showing rhizoidal attachment of thallus to rock and in sand; (B) several plants as seen when the thalli are flattened and closely associated with each other; (C) magnified view of alga showing the large polygonal cells.

Valonia ventricosa J. Agardh

Beachcombers along the Florida coast occasionally find what look like green grapes indiscriminately discarded on the sand by a thoughtless picnicker. Close inspection, however, might reveal the "garbage" to be individual plants of *V. ventricosa* which are about the same size, color, and texture as California white grapes.

This alga normally grows attached to rocks and ledges in shallow water, but it frequently breaks loose and is washed up on the beach. Each plant generally consists of one large oval to spherical-shaped light green cell (vesicle) with a small rhizoidal holdfast at the base. Colonies of the alga may occur, but usually the plants are solitary and do not form clusters. It is reported that in the West Indies individual vesicles may reach the size of a small hen's egg.

The vesicles remain turgid as long as they are submerged, but upon drying they become wrinkled and compressed. When fresh they burst easily if squeezed and pop if stepped upon. They are of no known economic value but are of interest to biologists because of the large coenocytic cells.

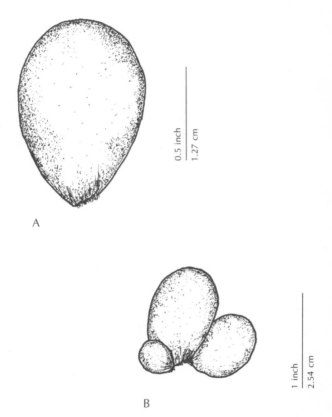

0.5 inch
1.27 cm

1 inch
2.54 cm

A

B

Valonia ventricosa—(A) single plant; (B) three-celled colony.

Field Notes

The Brown Algae

Division *Phaeophycophyta*

Gr. *phaios*, brown + *phykos*,
seaweed + *phyton*, plant

No other group of algae exhibits the range in form, size, or complexity of structure as do the members of this division. In addition, no other group is so strictly marine. Of the more than 1,500 known species, less than 1% occur in fresh water.

Brown algae range in size from microscopic filamentous forms less than $1/16$ inch in length to massive plants up to 300 feet long. Internally, some of these larger forms, called kelps, have a high degree of tissue complexity. As yet, no unicellular, colonial, or unbranched filamentous species have been described.

A few genera of *Phaeophycophyta* are entirely restricted to warm seas, but in general the brown algae show maximum development, both in size and number of species, in the colder waters of both the northern and southern hemispheres. The typical color of these plants, a rich brown, is attributed to the presence of an accessory pigment called *fucoxanthin* which masks the presence of the green photosynthetic chlorophyll.

Economically, this group of algae is very important. Several species are processed for human consumption, especially in the Orient, and brown algae have been used extensively for fertilizer. Commercially, the extraction of algin, a cell wall component, constitutes a large and growing industry. The salts of algin are known as alginates and have wide use in the manufacture of soaps, paints, leather finishers, insecticides, toothpastes, lipsticks, and medicines, as stabilizers in food products, and as clarifying agents in the production of beers. As part of the marine flora brown algae provide food, shelter, spawning areas, and a substrate for numerous marine animals.

Ectocarpus Lyngbye

This genus is well represented along the Atlantic coast with at least ten species described for a variety of localities from Baffin Bay to the Caribbean. The species are separated on the basis of microscopic characters such as gametangial appearance and position. Macroscopically they can be superficially separated using overall size and degree of filament entanglement as guidelines, but these characters by themselves will not ordinarily delimit more than one or two species.

Plants are a yellowish to dark brown color, much branched, and filamentous in construction. Large colonies are frequently encountered growing as epiphytes on coarser algae or growing en masse on floating debris or on solid objects such as dock pilings, stones, and other outcroppings in shallow waters.

Because of the filamentous nature of these algae, they perhaps can best be described as bushy or hairlike tufts of soft, brownish colored, stringy entanglements. They exhibit a delicate attractive display when submerged, but upon removal from the water form an amorphous, unattractive, somewhat slimy mat. Little is known about their usefulness as food for marine fauna, but because of their extensively branched thalli they undoubtedly provide shelter and protection for numerous small animals.

Two commonly encountered species are described on the following pages.

Ectocarpus confervoides (Roth) Le Jolis

Geographically distributed from Baffin Island to Florida, *E. confervoides* is quite variable in appearance, and as a consequence several varieties and forms are recognized. In general, however, the alga can be described as tufted, 2 to 12 inches tall, and growing on other algae, marine phanerogams, or submerged objects. It is dark brown to greenish brown and frequently can be found in extensive masses along shorelines, either as drift or as an epiphyte on seed plants in shallow water.

The filaments are long, much branched, and slightly entangled. In some instances the brown pigments are not abundant and the plants, then exhibiting an olive green coloration, might be mistaken for a species of *Cladophora*. Microscopically, however, there is little similarity between the two. Fruiting bodies (gametangia and sporangia) may be found the year around.

Ectocarpus confervoides—habit sketch of plant growing on stolon of eelgrass.

Ectocarpus dasycarpus Kuckuck

This species occurs along the coast of Rhode Island and Massachusetts. It typically grows in tufts, 2 to 3 inches tall, on coarser algae and phanerogams. At times the colonies almost completely cover the plant axes on which they are growing. Color is a light brown.

Individual filaments are only slightly entangled even though they are profusely branched. When removed from the water the tufts are slimy in appearance. Gametangia and sporangia are produced in early summer.

2 inches
5.08 cm

Ectocarpus dasycarpus—colonies of the alga growing on the stipes of *Laminaria* species.

Pylaiella littoralis (L.) Kjellman

Easily mistaken for *Ectocarpus* or *Cladophora*, this alga is a common inhabitant of shallow water, including brackish, from New Jersey northward. It grows in tufted colonies on rocks, coarser algae, and other submerged objects.

Although a brown alga and generally a light brown to greenish brown color, the thallus may, depending on growing conditions, be completely green in which case the resemblance to *Cladophora* is great. Microscopically, the alga can be readily identified because the gametangia and sporangia form intercalary series, a condition not found in the other two genera, but this character is of no use for field identification.

Filamentous and profusely branched, the alga grows erect and may be 18 or more inches tall. Frequently the filaments are twisted into thick ropelike strands, and when the plant is removed from the water the entangled filaments form dense, unattractive mats. Rhizoidal filaments anchor the alga to the substratum.

The thallus varies considerably in appearance from locality to locality, and because of this several varieties and forms have been recognized. Little is known of the extent to which this alga is used as food by marine animals, but the soft texture of the filaments makes its use seem likely.

1 inch

2.54 cm

Pylaiella littoralis—tufts of this alga frequently colonize coarser algae such as *Ascophyllum nodosum*.

Dictyopteris membranacea (Stackhouse) Batters

The flattened, thin, almost transparent blades, the prominent thick midribs, and the dichotomous branching make identification of this alga rather easy. The blades are strap-shaped and slightly tapered above, the midrib often denuded near the base. Conspicuous dots of clustered sterile hairs speckle the thallus, which is characteristically a light brown or brownish green color.

The alga can be found growing on rocks at low tide along the coast of North Carolina, the only reported location along the Atlantic coast of the United States, although the range is probably much larger. Plants are frequently brought up by dredges working in Bogue Inlet off Beaufort, North Carolina, the specimens often massive, bushy, and up to 12 inches in height. Individual blade segments may measure ½ inch or more in width. A rhizoidal holdfast fastens the plant to the substratum.

Small invertebrates colonize these plants and the thalli may serve as food for some animals. In Hawaii, species of *Dictyopteris* are used for human consumption.

1 inch
———
2.54 cm

Dictyopteris membranacea—habit sketch of plant showing the conspicuous midribs, dichotomous branching, and clusters (dots) of sterile hairs.

Dictyota ciliolata Kützing

The light brown color and the regular dichotomous branching of the thallus make this alga one of the most attractive plants found along the Florida coast. Fresh specimens, if whole and not shredded by wave action, exhibit almost perfect paired branches heightened in beauty by tiny teeth along the blade margins. Unlike *Dictyopteris* there are no midveins.

Individual plants may reach a height of about 6 inches growing erect from a fibrous holdfast. Branch segments vary from ¼ to ½ inch in width and may be spirally twisted in bushy plants. The alga typically grows on rocks in fairly shallow water but is frequently encountered as drift.

Distribution is restricted to warmer climates, from Florida southward. In the Pacific Islands several species of *Dictyota* are utilized as food by the natives.

1 inch
2.54 cm

Dictyota ciliolata—a single plant showing the dichotomous branching and toothed margins of the blades.

Padina vickersiae Hoyt   Potato Chip Alga

In shallow waters of protected places along the Florida coast one frequently finds blade segments of *P. vickersiae*, which, because of their thin,
somewhat ruffled, fan-shaped appearance and light brown color, do indeed remind one of potato chips. The segments may be lightly calcified
and are distinctly zonate, emphasizing the appropriateness of the common name given this alga.

Whole plants form tufts up to 6 inches in height with fanlike blades,
segmented at the margins, arising from short, fibrous stalks. Holdfasts are
bulbous and rhizoidal. The alga is characteristically associated with mangrove roots and submerged rocks, shells, or coral fragments and is common in occurrence.

The thalli can easily be mistaken for several other closely related genera, but close inspection of the blades reveals an inrolled margin, which is
distinctive. Depending upon the degree of calcification the alga may be
whitish brown or tan. The conspicuous ringlike bands of the blade are due
to alternate zones of hair-covered and glabrous regions.

Padina vickersiae is a warm-water alga found along our Atlantic coast
from North Carolina southward. It has no known commercial value, and
the extent to which it might be used as food by marine fauna is not known.
Its aesthetic value cannot be denied.

1 inch

2.54 cm

Padina vickersiae—The zonation of the blades and the inrolled blade margin are distinctive for this alga.

Zonaria tournefortii (Lamouroux) Montagne

Drift specimens of Z. *tournefortii* may be found washed ashore along the coast of North Carolina, but the plant is typically a deep-water alga. It is commonly dredged, unintentionally, by boats working off the Carolina coast and in Bogue Inlet. It may very well be that much of the drift material found originates in this way, since the holdfasts are usually missing.

The color of the alga is light chocolate to reddish brown, occasionally greenish brown, with much-branched flattened blades originating from rather substantial stipes. The lower parts of the branches are stemlike and continue for short distances into the lamina as midveins. Faint concentric zonations can be found near the blade margins. Blade segments are fan-shaped distally.

Mature plants are bushy, growing erect from a felted rhizoidal holdfast and reaching a height of 6 or 7 inches. Both blade and stipe are frequently encrusted with bryozoans and other small invertebrates. Whether the thalli are eaten by any marine animals is not known with certainty but it seems likely. The bushiness of the alga provides refuge and shelter for numerous small fish and other sea creatures.

1 inch
2.54 cm

Zonaria tournefortii—habit sketch of a plant showing the fan-shaped blades and the stipe. Bryozoans encrust portions of the blades.

Elachistea fucicola (Velley) Areschoug

From New Jersey northward this epiphytic alga is common, occurring as individual tufts or as extensive felted masses on the blades and stipes of coarser algae such as *Fucus* and *Ascophyllum*. When growing on fucoids the contrast in colors is striking, *E. fucicola* a yellowish brown color and the rockweed usually a deep, rich, chocolate brown or reddish brown color. The close association with *Fucus* accounts for the specific epithet.

Each tuft of the epiphyte consists of filaments up to ½ inch in length originating from a dense, filamentous cushion closely adherent to the host plant. The basal filaments actually penetrate the host tissues, but this is not apparent macroscopically. It is unlikely that the epiphyte damages the host in any way, although when particularly abundant it may completely cover the blade and thereby restrict photosynthesis.

Elachistea fucicola is not an attractive alga, and its presence on coarser algae does not enhance their appearance. The filamentous nature of the thalli may, however, attract small invertebrates and serve as a food source. Another species, *E. minutissima* Taylor, is epiphytic within the tiny cryptostomata of *Sargassum*, a warm-water brown alga.

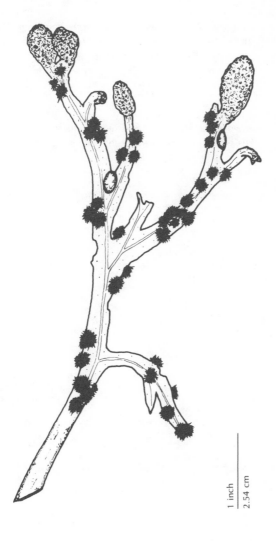

1 inch
2.54 cm

Elachistea fucicola—colonies of this alga frequently grow as epiphytes on *Fucus* species.

Leathesia difformis (L.) Areschoug

This alga is an epiphyte usually found on coarser algae such as *Chondrus crispus* and *Gracilaria verrucosa* and is often found washed ashore, occasionally littering sheltered beach areas. It is conspicuous and readily recognized because of its shape, which ranges from convolute spherical or irregular lobed masses to grape-sized hollow spheres. Individual thalli may reach a diameter of 3 to 4 inches. Except for the habitat and color, which varies from light brown to yellow-brown or olive, the plant strongly resembles the genus *Valonia* of the tropics, but since the geographical distributions of the two do not overlap, they should not be confused. *Leathesia difformis* occurs from North Carolina north to Nova Scotia and Newfoundland.

Structurally, the alga is filamentous but this is not evident macroscopically except perhaps at the basal point of attachment. In addition to *Gracilaria* and *Chondrus*, an association with coralline algae is often seen, pieces of which may be found attached to drift specimens.

Leathesia has no known economic significance.

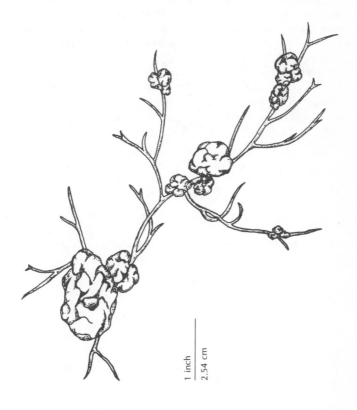

1 inch
―――――
2.54 cm

Leathesia difformis—colonies of the alga growing on a sprig of
Gracilaria verrucosa.

Ralfsia verrucosa (Areschoug) J. Agardh   Tarspot

Common names for plants are sometimes more descriptive than are lengthy lists of characteristics. This is perhaps the case with *R. verrucosa*, for the alga might indeed be mistaken for a tarspot, especially when growing on a submerged rock.

The plants, when young, form flat crusts closely adherent to the substratum and difficult to detach. With age they become brittle and more loosely attached, but still are not easily separated from the rocks, shells, or coarser algae on which they might be growing. The color is dark brown to blackish. Mature plants may reach a diameter of up to 4 inches.

The thalli are filamentous and two layered, the basal filaments radiating from a central point and in close contact with the substratum; the upper filaments are erect and laterally united, forming a compact surface.

The alga is found along the coast of New Jersey and northward, common in tidepools and on intertidal rocks. It is of no known economic value.

1 inch
2.54 cm

Ralfsia verrucosa—typical habitat and appearance of the tarspot alga.

Desmotrichum undulatum (J. Agardh) Reinke

The species is epiphytic, usually found growing on the leaves of eelgrass (*Zostera marina*). The alga consists of several light brown, linear-shaped blades spreading from a disclike holdfast. The blades are spirally twisted and membranous, ⅛ to ¾ inch in width and from 1 to 2 inches in length. The contrast in color between the dark green leaf of *Zostera* and the light brown color of the alga is striking.

Each blade of the thallus is unbranched, tapered at the base as well as the apex, making identification relatively easy. Distribution is from New Jersey northward.

The soft-textured blades of the alga probably serve as a food source for marine fauna, but little is known about this. In some *Zostera* beds the alga may be abundant, especially in early summer, providing additional niches of refuge for small fish and invertebrates seeking to escape from predators.

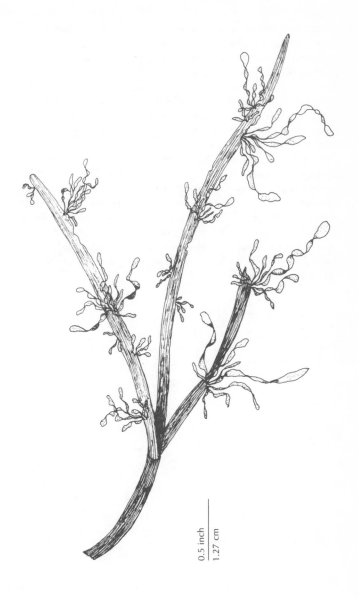

0.5 inch
1.27 cm

Desmotrichum undulatum—the spirally twisted blades of this epiphytic alga are distinctive. Eelgrass is the common host for the alga.

Petalonia fascia (O.F. Müller) Kuntze

Although primarily a northern species, *P. fascia* has been reported from North Carolina and Florida and from as far south as Brazil. Northern distribution extends to Newfoundland and Baffin Island. Several varieties have been described, which is not surprising considering its wide distribution.

The thallus is composed of flat, ribbon-shaped blades up to 17 inches in length. The blades are slightly tapered at the apices and at the base form slender stalks which terminate in small disclike holdfasts. Color varies from a dark brown to a greenish brown.

The alga is typically found attached to stones and rocks near the high-tide level and may be found in estuaries. In appearance it resembles *Desmotrichum undulatum* and small plants might be mistaken for that species, but the blades of *P. fascia* are longer, thicker, and less curled. In addition, *D. undulatum* is epiphytic, usually on eelgrass, whereas *P. fascia* is only rarely found growing on other plants and then generally on fucoids.

Because of the membranous blades this alga would seem to be an ideal food plant for marine animals, but to what extent it might be used for this purpose remains to be disclosed.

1 inch
2.54 cm

Petalonia fascia—habit sketch of alga showing the flat, ribbon-shaped blades, slender stipes, and small holdfasts.

Scytosiphon lomentaria
(Lyngbye) C. Agardh

Sea Sausage

The erect tubular thallus, regularly constricted at intervals in mature plants, gives *S. lomentaria* the appearance of sausage links. The common name, therefore, is quite appropriate. The thalli reach their largest size in cold northern waters, but the alga is distributed from Labrador to Bermuda with collections from Maine, Massachusetts, and Delaware south to Florida.

The fronds are cylindrical, unbranched, hollow at maturity, and up to 2 feet or more in length, although warm-water specimens are generally much smaller. The thalli grow in erect clusters from small disc-shaped holdfasts. Being gregarious, the plants often form extensive colonies attached to rocks, shells, and other submerged objects at or below low tide. The color varies from a light brown to a greenish brown or yellow-brown.

No economic importance is attached to this alga, but extensive colonies of the plant provide convenient shelter for small fishes, and the thalli contribute nicely to the often bizarre appearance of marine communities. Quite likely the alga is grazed by some marine animals.

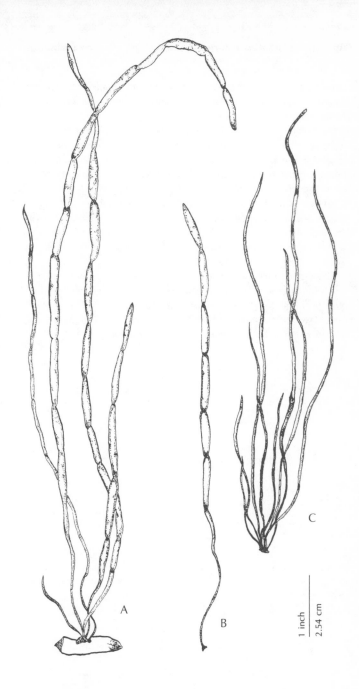

Scytosiphon lomentaria—(A) colony of mature plants showing growth habit; (B) single plant showing the inflated, constricted, tubular thallus and the small, disc-shaped holdfast; (C) juvenile plants with cylindrical, nonconstricted fronds.

Agarum cribrosum (Mertens) Bory   Sea Colander

One of the prettiest of brown algae in this author's opinion, A. cribrosum is easily recognized because of the perforate blade, the feature responsible for the common name colander.

Expanding from a short, slender stalk, the wrinkled blade is somewhat heart-shaped at its base, broadens to a width of 20 or more inches, and lengths of 3 to 4 feet have been seen in deep water. A stout, somewhat leathery, highly compressed midvein extends from the stipe to the blade apex. The color ranges from a deep brown to a light chocolate brown.

When seen for the first time the alga might appear to the collector to be weatherbeaten or severely chewed by marine animals. The perforations in the blade are natural, however, and are found in attached specimens as well as those washed ashore. Attachment is to rocks and large shells by means of stout fibrous holdfasts.

Although characteristically a deep-water plant, sea colander is commonly found growing in exposed tide pools in association with kelps and other brown algae. The geographical distribution of the species extends from Massachusetts northward. The alga is of no known economic value other than the part it plays in the biological food chain.

2 inches
5.08 cm

Agarum cribrosum—habit sketch of alga showing the perforated blade, prominent midrib, and stout holdfast.

Alaria esculenta (L.) Greville   Winged Kelp

The winged kelp is fairly common along northern rocky coasts from Massachusetts to Labrador and Baffin Island. It is especially common to exposed rocky shorelines where strong tidal currents and a strong surf are the rule rather than the exception. A subtidal alga, it grows attached to submerged rocks, shells, or other objects by means of a stout, branched, fibrous holdfast.

The plant is easily recognized by the conspicuous midrib, strongly compressed, which runs the entire length of the vegetative blade. The blade is unbranched, up to 10 or more inches in width, and 10 to 12 feet in length. A slender cylindrical stipe, up to 1 foot long, flattens toward the apex into a fertile rachis which bears numerous, pinnately arranged, spatula-shaped blades (sporophylls) 3 to 10 inches long and ½ to 1½ inches wide. The vegetative blade is produced terminally on the rachis. Color ranges from a dark brown to an olive green or yellow-brown depending on the depth at which the alga is growing.

In parts of Ireland and Scotland this alga is used for food, especially the "fingers" (sporophylls) and the "sweet" midrib stripped of its membranous margins. In the United States it is not known to be used for any particular purpose.

Alaria esculenta—(A) growth habit of two plants showing the conspicuous midrib and pinnately arranged sporophylls; (B) sporophylls showing fertile areas.

Chorda Stackhouse

Two species of the genus *Chorda* are found along the Atlantic coast. Both are cold-water annuals geographically distributed from New Jersey and Long Island north to Labrador and the Arctic.

The genus is easily recognized, as the thallus in both species is cylindrical, relatively small in diameter, and often of considerable length. Attachment is by means of a small, disclike holdfast which appears entirely incapable of holding the alga in place, yet is highly efficient since the plants are frequently found growing in strong tidal currents. Superficial resemblance to twine, smooth or frayed rope, or tough cord is remarkable.

Color varies from dark brown to light brown or greenish brown. Occasionally bright green specimens are found, but close inspection usually reveals some portion of the thallus to be of typical brown coloration.

No economic use has been reported for either species, but aesthetic value cannot be denied since either or both species, in association with kelps and smaller brown and red algae, add immensely to the beauty of marine communities.

Chorda filum (L.) Lamouroux

Sea Twine,
Devil's Shoelace

Mature plants of *C. filum* are smooth and very slippery in contrast to the hairy appearance of *C. tomentosa*. Young plants, however, have a coating of fine colorless hairs, which are gradually lost as the plants age.

A small irregular holdfast terminates a slender stipe which expands distally into the upper portion of the thallus, the latter about ½ inch in diameter or larger. Length of the plant is reportedly up to 30 feet, tapering toward the apex.

The species is common, growing in clumps on stones and shells in subtidal areas. Mature portions of the thallus are hollow, giving the plant some buoyancy and a semierect growth habit. Fruiting occurs in late summer.

6 inches

15.2 cm

Chorda filum—habit sketch of several plants showing the very long, cylindrical, unbranched thalli and tiny disc-shaped holdfasts.

Chorda tomentosa Lyngbye

This species, generally 3 to 4 feet in length but reportedly reaching a length of 20 or more feet, is immediately recognizable because the ropelike thallus is covered with short, free filaments which give it a hairy appearance. A slender smooth stipe, approximately an inch long, is basally attached by means of a small disc-shaped holdfast. The upper portion of the thallus is about ¼ inch in diameter, but because of the filaments may appear much thicker when the plant is submerged. The alga is slippery in texture and is characteristically a plant of the spring flora, fruiting in late spring. Attachment is to smooth surfaces such as rocks and shells at and below low tide.

1 foot

30.4 cm

Chorda tomentosa—habit sketch of alga as it is seen submerged.
The hairs are conspicuous only when the thallus is in the water.

Laminaria Lamouroux

Several species of this genus are found in abundance along our northeastern coast where, along with other large brown algae, they are referred to as kelp. The species are characteristically cold-water plants with a distribution spreading northward from Connecticut and Rhode Island.

Among the largest seaweeds, the species are readily recognized by their well differentiated thallus, which always consists of a fibrous or disc-shaped holdfast, a slender, stemlike stipe, and a blade which may or may not be divided into segments. The plants are generally leathery in texture and light brown to chocolate brown in color. They grow attached to rocks, pilings, wharfs, shells, and other submerged objects, but frequently are washed ashore where they are conspicuous because of their size and color. Beaches may literally be covered with fragments and sometimes whole specimens of *Laminaria* following a storm.

Formerly an important source of iodine and potash, but now infrequently harvested for that purpose, species of *Laminaria* are still of considerable economic value as a food source in the Orient. Dried *Laminaria* is known as Kombu in Japan and is consumed in sauces and soups, eaten as a vegetable, or cooked with meat. In China Kombu is known as Haita and is often stewed with pork. *Laminaria* is sometimes used as a substitute for tea, and when candied it is used as a confectionary. Stipes of the algae, exceedingly hard when dried, are sometimes fashioned into handles for knives and similar instruments, and coastal farmers have used kelp for fertilizer on their fields.

Laminaria agardhii Kjellman   Kelp

This species of *Laminaria* is conspicuous along our Atlantic coast from New Jersey to southern Massachusetts. It is the dominant kelp south of Cape Cod, occurring only sporadically northward from Massachusetts to Maine and into the Arctic.

The plants are often large, up to 10 feet in length, with a blade nearly a foot in width. The tip of the blade is often worn and frayed. The ruffled margin of the strap-shaped lamina is distinctive during spring and summer growth. A perennial plant, the blade is thick and flat during the winter season.

Attached to rocks, wharfs, jetties, and frequently mussels by a much-branched tough holdfast and a cylindrical stipe of variable length, depending upon depth, the species frequently forms massive colonies along exposed shores. The tenacious holdfast, flexible stipe, and rubbery blade make the plant especially resistant to the strong surf common to the rocky

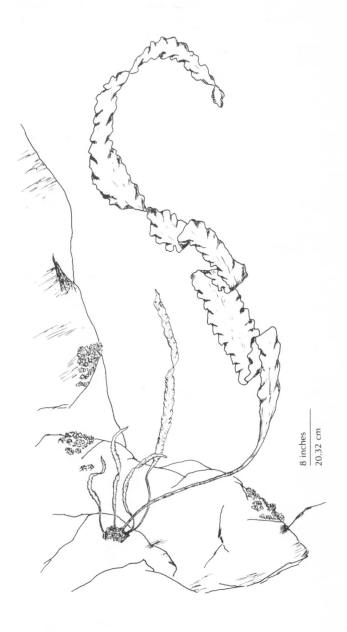

8 inches
20.32 cm

Laminaria agardhii—colony of plants showing characteristic ruffled margins of the blades.

New England coast. Juvenile plants can frequently be found in abundance in tide pools.

Fruiting normally occurs in winter with dark patches of reproductive cells developing on the blade. The alga might easily be mistaken for *Laminaria saccharina*, another kelp common to the area, but the latter has mucilage canals in the blade whereas *L. agardhii* does not. Some workers are of the opinion that the two algae are so similar that they might best be considered one species with varieties.

Laminaria saccharina (L.) Lamouroux — Sweet Tangle, Broadleaf Kelp

The specific epithet *saccharina* means "sugar" or "sweet substance" and refers to a white, powdery carbohydrate which accumulates on the surface of the blade of this kelp when it dries. The substance is sweet to the taste and, although found also on a number of other seaweeds, has for one reason or another become associated with this particular kelp.

Resembling *L. agardhii* rather closely in overall appearance, this alga is distributed from the north shore of Cape Cod to Newfoundland, Labrador, and Baffin Island. Whereas *L. agardhii* is the predominant kelp south of Cape Cod, *L. saccharina* is more common to the north. In addition, sweet tangle has mucilage canals in the blade while *L. agardhii* does not, but some phycologists are of the opinion that this is not a character of sufficient importance to warrant the recognition of two separate species.

The undivided blade of this kelp, like that of *L. agardhii*, becomes ruffled with age. In autumn the blade thickens and becomes leathery. The plants are moderately large and attached to rocks and shells by a much-branched holdfast. The stipe varies in length, but is shorter than the blade, which may reach a length of 6 feet.

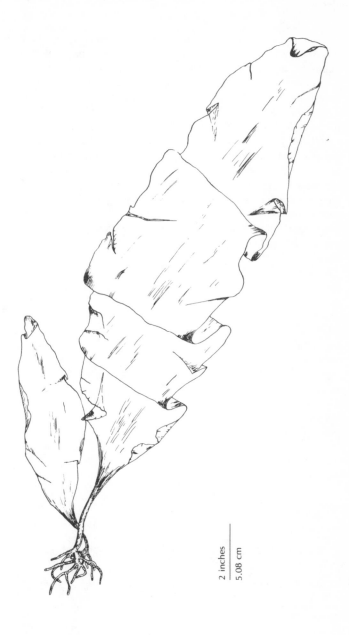

2 inches
5.08 cm

Laminaria saccharina—habit sketch of two plants. This alga closely resembles *L. agardhii*.

Laminaria digitata
(L.) Lamouroux

Tangle, Seastaff,
Sea Girdle, Horsetail

Often exceeding 6 feet in length, this seaweed may be found from Long Island northward to the Hudson Bay region. It becomes common north of Cape Cod, showing a preference for colder waters. The blade at maturity is segmented into strap-shaped lengths, giving the alga a distinctive appearance and accounting for at least one of its common names, horsetail.

The plants are often so securely fastened to large boulders or shells by means of the branched, fibrous holdfast that a knife is necessary to cut them loose. The stipe is cylindrical toward the base and much flattened and expanded near the blade. Cross sections of older stipes show concentric growth rings, but cutting them to see these can be difficult, for in addition to being rubbery they may be tough and somewhat hardened, especially near the holdfast. The blade segments are leathery, quite enduring, and often several feet in length.

Laminaria digitata is perennial, fruiting in the winter.

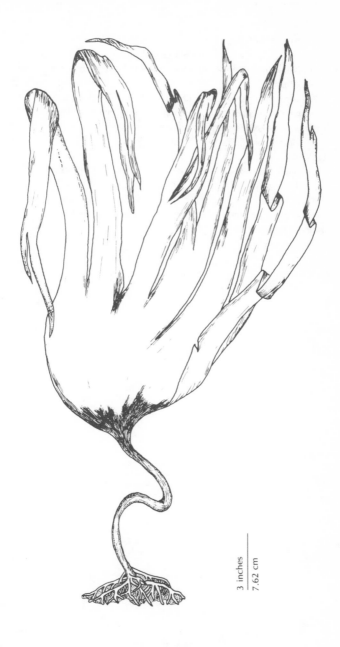

3 inches
7.62 cm

Laminaria digitata—habit sketch of a plant. The segmented blade, cylindrical stipe, and stout holdfast make identification of this seaweed rather easy.

Laminaria platymeris De la Pylaie

Kelp

The broad, shovel-shaped, moderately divided blade, flattened stipe, and dark brown color are all characteristic features of this kelp, although internally the presence of mucilage canals in both the blade and stipe is also distinctive.

The alga may reach a size of 5 to 6 feet in length, attached to the substratum by a coarse, much-branched, fibrous holdfast. At maturity the leathery blade is divided into broad segments which vary in number, three or five being typical. The stipe is flattened from the holdfast to the base of the lamina.

The plant is believed to be an annual frequenting deep water but often washed ashore where it becomes entangled among the boulders at low tide, the holdfast catching and holding in rock crevices. It is distributed from northern Massachusetts to Newfoundland and is fairly common around Mt. Desert Island, Maine.

2.5 inches

6.35 cm

Laminaria platymeris—the shovel-shaped blade of this alga is distinctive.

One of the most conspicuous and largest seaweeds found along our New England coast, *L. longicruris* is also one of the easiest kelps to identify on sight because of its distinctive stipe. The blade, which is undivided and somewhat ruffled along the margins, is attached to a cylindrical stipe which is solid near the holdfast but expanded and hollow in the upper portion. Where blade and stipe meet, the latter is much inflated and swollen.

The blade may reach a width of 2 to 4 feet and a length of 20 feet. The stipe, depending upon the depth of the water in which the alga is growing, may be 10 feet or more in length. Thus this kelp may reach an overall size of 30 or more feet. Attachment, usually to rocks, boulders, or large shells, is by means of a tough, much-branched holdfast.

Common from Rhode Island north to the Hudson Bay area, drifting plants are frequently seen off the coast of Maine where, because of their size and the swollen portion of the stipe, which protrudes from the water, they cannot pass unnoticed. Fragments and even whole specimens frequently wash ashore, the heavy surf tearing the plants from their place of attachment. Dislodged individuals are commonly found entangled in beach debris or caught in rock crevices during low tide.

1 foot
30.4 cm

Laminaria longicruris—habit sketch of a single plant showing the rather small holdfast compared to the overall size of the plant, the inflated distal portion of the stipe, and the fertile area of the blade.

Ascophyllum nodosum
(L.) Le Jolis

Rockweed, Knotted
Wrack, Yellow Wrack,
Knobbed Wrack, Sea
Whistle

From New Jersey northward (and occasionally as drift in more southern locations) this seaweed is one of the most common of intertidal algae. Often it occurs in such abundance as to completely cover rocks exposed at low tide. In combination with other rockweeds (*Fucus* species) this alga forms a distinct zonation of plant life along rocky shorelines with the wrack concentrated in the zone closest to the water's edge at low tide. It was once harvested as a source of iodine and has been used extensively as "green manure." The fact that it is so common and so well known probably accounts for its many and varied common names.

Individual plants may reach a length of 8 to 10 feet. They grow erect and somewhat spreading from a disc-shaped holdfast. The main axis is generally compressed and oval in section. Branching is irregular. Thick-walled air bladders, oval in shape, occur singly and are abundant along the branches. Color of the plant varies from a rich brown to olive green or yellow. Fruiting occurs in winter and early spring with the appearance of warty swollen receptacles. These are deciduous and are shed in late spring. The sterile summer plants are therefore very different in appearance from the fruiting plants.

The profuse growth of *A. nodosum* over rock surfaces provides, under the protective fronds, a moist shelter for many marine animals which otherwise could not survive the rigors of the intertidal habitat.

2 inches
5.08 cm

A   B

Ascophyllum nodosum—habit sketches. (A) vegetative plant; (B) fruiting plant showing receptacles.

Fucus Linnaeus Rockweed

Species of *Fucus*, along with those of *Ascophyllum*, are known as rockweeds by coastal residents. The name is quite appropriate, especially for *Fucus* species, as the plants are associated with intertidal rocky areas from North Carolina to northern Canada. If any one seaweed is most likely to be encountered by the casual visitor to the northeastern Atlantic coast, *Fucus* would likely be that seaweed. It can be found on almost every rocky outcropping, stone piling, jetty, or discarded brick found between low and high tide levels.

Although *Fucus* plants are easy to recognize and distinguish from other brown algae, the problem of species identification is not always easy. Mature specimens are usually needed for positive identification, since the gross appearance of the fruiting structures (receptacles), the presence or absence of air bladders, and the microscopic determination of sexuality are diagnostic features. Juvenile plants of the several species look very much alike, and the presence or absence of air bladders may be due to environmental conditions. Thus the absence of bladders may or may not be significant.

In general, a *Fucus* plant can be recognized quickly. The holdfast is disc-shaped or slightly irregular, but always small compared to the size of the plant it anchors and much like a suction cup. The axis branches dichotomously, forming readily visible pairs or "Y's." Each branch, as well as the main axis, has a distinct midrib, although in the lower portions of the plant this may be indistinct due to the narrowing blades. The receptacles are terminal on main branches, swollen, or in some species conspicuously compressed, but always warty or knobby in appearance. If air bladders are present they are frequently numerous, and generally in pairs with one on each side of the midrib. Color varies from light brown to dark brown or olive green. Secretion of a slimy mucus is characteristic and especially noticeable with freshly collected specimens, which invariably are slippery.

Of the five species reported from our Atlantic coast, three are very common and are described in this manual.

Fucus edentatus De la Pylaie Rockweed

Distributed from New Jersey northward but uncommon south of Cape Cod, this species is readily identified if fruiting by the compressed, extremely elongated receptacles. Frequently branched dichotomously, and not much thicker than the branches bearing them, the receptacles are several times longer than broad and warty in appearance. There are no air bladders.

The plants are of moderate size, generally 10 to 15 inches long, although larger specimens have been recorded. They grow erect from a

Fucus edentatus—the elongated, compressed, often branched receptacles are distinctive.

somewhat broadened disc-shaped holdfast. The midvein is not as conspicuous as in some of the other species of *Fucus*. The alga is attached to rocks in the intertidal zone and fruits in late winter and spring, the receptacles often identifiable through summer. Color is generally a dark brown.

Fucus spiralis L.   Rockweed

Despite the sometimes twisted or spiral nature of the branches of this species, the alga is not easily distinguished from *F. vesiculosus*. Indeed, a specimen of the latter, if lacking air bladders as is frequently the case, is practically identical to *F. spiralis*. About the only way to make a positive identification is by a determination of sexuality. In *F. spiralis* both male and female sex cells are produced by the same plant. In *F. vesiculosus* the plants are male or female producing one type of gamete only. This characteristic is difficult to determine without microscopic examination of receptacle contents. However, if air bladders are present on the plant being examined it is definitely *F. vesiculosus*, not *F. spiralis*.

The receptacles of this species are swollen and when mature frequently have a ridge which encircles the receptacle in the plane of the blade. The ridge is not always conspicuous, however, and therefore is not a reliable characteristic.

Individual plants have a tendency to be bushy, reach a length of 8 to 12 inches, and branch freely. The midribs of the upper branches are quite evident. The holdfast is comparatively small and conical. Receptacles are oval to oblong, swollen, warty looking, and frequently forked. Air bladders are never present.

Distribution of the species is from Delaware northward, usually high in the intertidal zone, i.e., above the zone of *F. vesiculosus* and *Ascophyllum nodosum*.

1 inch
2.54 cm

Fucus spiralis—habit sketch of plant showing the somewhat spirally twisted branches and the "rough-hewn" receptacles with encircling ridges.

Fucus vesiculosus L.   Rockweed, Bladder Wrack,
                                Lady Wrack, Sea Ware,
                                Black Tang, Bladder Fucus

The specific epithet in this binomial refers to the vesicles or air bladders which are characteristic of the plant. However, the production of bladders seems to be related to environmental conditions, and consequently they may or may not be present. Plants growing in fully exposed sites and subject to strong currents or surf might not have vesicles, whereas those growing in protected areas or quieter waters usually do have them. Thus this feature is not consistent. One can be assured, however, that if bladders are present in a *Fucus*, it is *F. vesiculosus*, for no other Atlantic coast species of the genus is vesiculate. If there are no bladders, the plant could be *F. vesiculosus* or *F. spiralis*, and only examination of the receptacle contents will determine which species it is (see p. 116).

The species is the most common of the genus, being distributed abundantly in the intertidal zone from North Carolina north to Hudson Bay. Any rocky area in this broad region is likely to have growths of the species. The bladders, if present, are usually paired with one on each side of the branch midrib. They may be few or many in number. In size they vary from small spherical structures to elongated swellings ½ inch or more in length. In freshly collected material they pop when squeezed.

Individual plants grow erect from a disc-shaped or irregularly lobed holdfast which is always small in comparison to the plant itself. The thalli are commonly 12 to 24 inches long, but may reach a length of several feet. The midribs are strongly evident, the receptacles greatly swollen and up to an inch in length. They frequently are forked and at maturity are warty in appearance, yielding copious amounts of mucilage if squashed while still fresh. Fruiting occurs throughout the winter season.

Fucus vesiculosus, as well as other species of rockweed, have in the past been used for the treatment of goiter and obesity, and on occasion as fertilizer. In the Western Hebrides the species is reported to be used as winter food for sheep and cattle.

1 inch
———
2.54 cm

Fucus vesiculosus—the paired air bladders are distinctive of the species. The receptacles are much swollen and the midribs are conspicuous.

Sargassum C. Agardh   Gulfweed

Species of *Sargassum* can be difficult to identify because of variability in
form and a reliance on such features as the presence or absence of
holdfasts, receptacles, and cryptostomata (tufts of hairs in minute cavities)
for positive identification. While these features are reliable and most useful to the botanist, they generally are of little value to the layman who finds
a sprig of *Sargassum* cast ashore on the beach and wants a quick identification.

Fortunately, the plants can be quickly recognized as belonging to the
genus *Sargassum* on the basis of more obvious and consistent characteristics. The genus is characterized by a conspicuous stemlike axis with
distinct foliar appendages superficially resembling the leaves of higher
plants. In addition, small berrylike air bladders occur in abundance and
usually can be found on even the smallest of fragments. Color is likewise
fairly consistent, the plants varying from yellow-brown to a deep rich
chocolate color. Seldom could fragments of *Sargassum* be mistaken for a
red or green alga.

Several of the most likely to be encountered species are described on
the following pages, but no attempt is made to include the multitude of
species that are known.

Sargassum filipendula C. Agardh   Gulfweed

From the tropics northward to Massachusetts, this seaweed is common on
rocks and shells from just below low-tide level to depths of 90 feet or
more. Attachment is by means of a disc-shaped or flattened, somewhat
lobed holdfast from which the erect, "leafy" axis arises. Individual plants
may reach a length of 2 to 3 feet, the strands buoyed up by spherical,
stalked bladders. The toothed "leaves" have prominent midribs and scat-
tered dotlike cryptostomata. Fruiting occurs in late summer and autumn.
The receptacles are smaller than the vegetative appendages and are clustered in the upper parts of the plant. The species is believed to be perennial.

Whenever *Sargassum* is mentioned, visions of the much publicized
Sargasso Sea, an immense lens-shaped mass of floating gulfweed in the
North Atlantic northeast of the West Indies, comes to mind. This contributes to the popular misconception that *Sargassum* is a tropical seaweed
found only in warm southern waters. While this is true for most of the
Atlantic coast species, it is not without exception. *Sargassum filipendula* is
one of these exceptions, since it is a common subtidal alga found off the
coast of Massachusetts. Other species of *Sargassum* are occasionally cast
ashore along our northern coast, especially after storms from the south-
east, having been carried north from the Caribbean by the Gulf Stream.
But *S. filipendula* is the only species which grows attached in our northern
waters, and any attached plant of *Sargassum* found in this area can be
120 identified as *S. filipendula*.

1.5 inches
3.81 cm

Sargassum filipendula—habit sketch of plant showing holdfast and growth form.

Sargassum fluitans Bøyesen and   Gulfweed
Sargassum natans (L.) J. Meyen

It has been reported that more than 90% (by bulk) of the gulfweed composing the Sargasso Sea is made up of two free-floating species, *S. fluitans* and *S. natans*. Neither of these is ever found attached, and both are sterile.

The formerly held view that these plants are fragments of weeds torn loose from vast submerged beds of *Sargassum* near the Azores has been rejected, since no such beds have ever been found. Nor, as some botanists have proposed, is there any evidence that the seaweed comes from banks in the West Indies or the Gulf of Mexico. It appears more likely that the two species grow, reproduce vegetatively, and live independently as pelagic plants, their accumulation in certain areas being the result of major current systems and the conveyance of water masses with different densities.

The two species look much alike in gross appearance, but close inspection reveals a projection or pointed tip on the air bladders of *S. natans* and no such structure on the bladders of *S. fluitans*. Other differences such as leaf shape, length of leaves, and leaf margin are significant, but due to variability in these characteristics it is difficult to use them unless one is experienced. Even the pointed tip of the bladder in *S. natans* is subject to modification and may on occasion be reduced and inconspicuous. Thus variability in this characteristic must also be recognized, and this makes positive identification even more difficult.

Identification of specimens found on a beach is a great challenge, since there is no way of knowing for sure whether they are fragments of attached plants or if, in the absence of fruiting structures, they might be capable of sexual reproduction but are immature. The task of identifying species of *Sargassum* is therefore a difficult one except for those who have studied the genus thoroughly. For the layman, a process of elimination is as positive an approach as any. If the individual plant in question has a holdfast or is fruiting, it is neither *S. fluitans* nor *S. natans*. If the specimen is known to be pelagic, then the possibility of its being one of the two species is good, and the vesicles can be examined for further identification. If pointed tips occur on the bladders, the plant is *S. natans*.

Absence of a dominant central axis, profuse branching, and entanglement of branches are characteristics which can also be associated with these two species. By themselves, however, these characteristics are not definitive.

Sargassum fluitans—habit sketch of thallus showing broad leaves and air bladders, noticeably without pointed tips.

Sargassum natans—habit sketch of alga showing the long, narrow leaves and the apiculate air bladders.

Sargassum pteropleuron Grunow   Gulfweed

This species of gulfweed grows attached to rocks and shells below low-tide levels in relatively shallow waters (10 to 12 feet). It resembles *S. filipendula* in gross appearance but it does not grow in deep water as does the latter, and it does not have the range of distribution of *S. filipendula*. Although common throughout the Caribbean, *S. pteropleuron* has not been reported north of Florida. *Sargassum filipendula*, on the other hand, is known as far north as southern Massachusetts as well as to the south where the distribution of the two species overlaps.

Two macroscopic characters, both somewhat variable, can be checked for species identification, although neither is totally reliable. The stems of *S. pteropleuron* are generally rough and warty, the air bladders short-stalked to almost sessile. In *S. filipendula* the bladders have slender stalks, up to ⅛ inch long, and the stems are smooth. Both species grow erect from a flattened, somewhat lobed holdfast, and both may exceed several feet in length. The leaves of *S. pteropleuron* tend to be somewhat longer and narrower than those of *S. filipendula*, but positive identifications are usually made only by those familiar with less obvious differences and *in toto* comparisons.

2 inches
5.08 cm

Sargassum pteropleuron—the rough, warty stem and the sessile air bladders are characteristic of this species. The leaves are long and narrow.

Turbinaria turbinata (L.) Kuntze

The specific epithet in this binomial means "top shaped" and refers to the swollen, peculiarly shaped leaves of the alga. Each leaf is pyramid-shaped with the tapered portion of the appendage forming a stalk by means of which the leaf is attached to the stem. The broadened part of the append- age faces away from the axis; thus each leaf is like an upside-down pyramid or a child's top. The older leaves contain an air sac so that functionally these appendages are similar to the air bladders of other brown algae, e.g., *Sargassum* species and *Fucus vesiculosus*. The color of the alga is generally a rich brown.

Individual plants grow erect from a much-branched fibrous holdfast and may reach a length of 12 inches or more. The alga is intertidal to subtidal, growing attached to rocks and coral reefs. Parts of plants or entire speci- mens are frequently washed ashore along with masses of *Sargassum*. The bizarre appearance of the plant never fails to attract and usually puzzle the beachcomber. Fruiting plants bear numerous forked receptacles in dense clusters. The receptacles are much smaller than the leaves, but are con- spicuous when present because of their abundance and vermiform shape.

Although *T. turbinata* may be found on beaches as far north as Cape Hatteras, the alga is native to the warmer waters of Florida and the Carib- bean. Other species of *Turbinaria* are reported to be eaten raw by the natives of Malaysia, have been made into pickles, and are used as fertilizer, particularly for coconut plantations, in India and the Philippines.

1 inch
2.54 cm

Turbinaria turbinata—habit sketch showing the distinctive in-flated leaves, growth form, and forked receptacles.

Field Notes

The Red Algae

Division *Rhodophycophyta*

Gr. *rhodon*, rose + *phykos*,
seaweed + *phyton*, plant

The algae in this division range in color from pink to rosy red to reddish purple. The red color is due to the presence of water-soluble pigments which mask the green photosynthetic chlorophyll. The abundance of these accessory pigments is related to light intensity: the stronger the light the weaker the red color. Thus, generally, the greater the depth at which the plant grows the darker its color. Drift specimens, fragmented and torn loose from attached plants, may exhibit various shades of red-green depending upon how long they have been floating at or near the surface. Finding totally green specimens is not uncommon. But even though the color of these seaweeds is not totally reliable for group recognition, little difficulty is generally encountered in separating the red algae from either the brown or green algae.

Of the approximately 4,000 known species of red seaweeds, about 98% are marine. They range in size from microscopic unicellular plants to fairly large macroscopic thalli. The plant body is basically filamentous, but compaction of cells may conceal this feature. Some species are delicate multifarious filaments, some form massive thin sheets, and many are coarse, cylindrical, and ropelike. The diversity of form makes the red algae, as a group, the most striking and beautiful of all seaweeds. Carefully mounted specimens are commonly used for Christmas cards, decorative stationery, and pictures. Homemade table mats and coasters with attractively arranged red, brown, and green seaweeds can be purchased at some coastal craft shops.

Rhodophycophyta occur in all latitudes, but are far more abundant in temperate and tropical waters than in the Arctic. They are also distributed from the highest of intertidal levels to the lowermost limits of light. The ability of the accessory pigments to absorb light of short wavelength and transfer the energy to the chlorophyll pigment accounts for the occurrence of these algae at great depths.

Economically, the red algae are of considerable importance. Agar-agar and carrageenin, gel-forming polysaccharides of wide usage, are extracted from several species of red seaweeds. In addition, a number of red algae are used as marine vegetables and eaten raw or in soups and sauces by people in many parts of the world. Like the brown and green algae, the red seaweeds are an important part of the food chain in marine waters.

131

Porphyra leucosticta Thuret and   Red Laver,
Porphyra umbilicalis (L.) J. Agardh   Purple Laver

Of the three species of *Porphyra* known to occur along our Atlantic coast, two are so common that they warrant inclusion in this guide. They are distinguishable from each other only on the basis of microscopic features (cell size and shape) and on the form and distribution of reproductive areas. The former characteristics are of no use in the field, and the latter are of use only during fruiting seasons. In gross appearance the two species look alike. Since their areas of distribution overlap and their appearance is similar, they are described here at the generic level with no attempt to delineate species.

The plants are membranous, forming broad sheetlike thalli strongly resembling sea lettuce (*Ulva lactuca*) except for color. Whereas the latter is some shade of green, species of *Porphyra* are purple-red to brownish purple or even reddish black. They are epiphytic on coarser algae or are attached to rocks, pilings, and shells. At high tide, when the thalli are submerged, they spread freely from a small holdfast and give the appearance of very delicate, easily torn, purple tissue-paper-like plants. At low tide they hang unglamorously as blackened, taut, and brittle sheets. With the return of the tide the plants swell, expand from their point of attachment, and become gelatinous and slippery to the touch. In this condition they are surprisingly tough and difficult to tear.

Porphyra leucosticta is found from Florida to Maine, growing on mangroves, *Fucus* stipes, and other coarse algae, as well as rocks at and above low-tide level. *Porphyra umbilicalis* is reported from as far south as Florida to the lower St. Lawrence-Hudson Bay region and Newfoundland. It grows abundantly on rocks and wharves.

Purple laver is an important food in the Orient, the Philippines, and Hawaii. It is consumed as food in Great Britain and Ireland and reportedly was a primary source of salt in the diet of the Indians populating our northwestern coastal states. Some species are cultivated in Japan, harvested, packaged as laver sheets, and distributed worldwide. The laver is used in soups and sandwiches, seasoned and eaten with rice, and used in the preparation of the famous Japanese Sushi. Some 4,000 to 5,000 metric tons (dry weight) of the alga are produced annually in Japan, and *Porphyra* seaweed farming is an integral part of Japanese agriculture. The value of this seaweed as a food source in the United States has yet to be realized.

1 inch
2.54 cm

Porphyra leucosticta—habit sketch of plant growing as an epiphyte on *Fucus spiralis*.

Asparagopsis hamifera (Hariot) Okamura

This very delicate, filamentous red alga is found as drift from the shores of Long Island Sound to southern Massachusetts. The thalli grow attached from just below low-tide level to considerable depths. They are most frequently encountered as fragments intermingled with, or entangled with, coarser algae awash in the tidal currents. Were it not for the rosy red color and peculiar hook-shaped branches which give the alga an unusual appearance, the fragments would probably go unnoticed. But when found in tangled masses or as fully spread loose fragments, the plants have the appearance of filamentous algae infested with sickle-shaped, ¼-inch-long roundworms. This usually attracts the attention of even the most casual observer.

Upon close inspection, *A. hamifera* is found to be a much-branched filamentous alga with branches becoming finer and finer toward the tips of the axes. The hook-shaped structures are recurved branch tips, which are conspicuous because they are larger than adjacent branch tips, are frequently strongly coiled, and may in diameter exceed the width of the main axis toward the base of the plant. By means of these hooks the alga is often attached to larger seaweeds.

The fineness of detail, the rosy red color, and the conspicuous hooks of this plant make it ideal as a collector's item for mounting. Even the size of the plant makes it perfect for this purpose, since attached specimens are seldom more than 3 to 4 inches in length. Fragments which are likely to be found cast ashore are even smaller.

One species, *A. sanfordiana* Harv., is consumed as food in Hawaii where it is known as Limu kohu. It is eaten as a relish or salad with fish, meat, and poi.

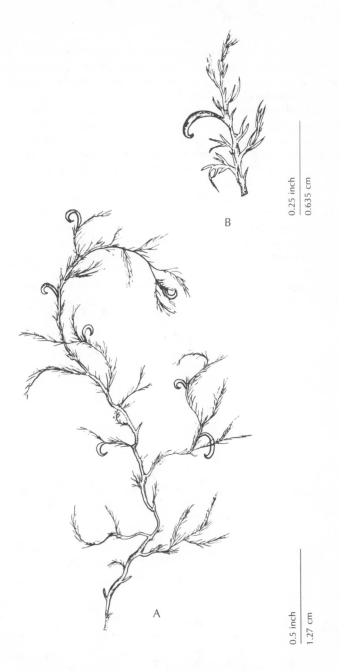

0.25 inch
0.635 cm

B

0.5 inch
1.27 cm

A

Asparagopsis hamifera—(A) habit sketch showing growth form and mode of branching; (B) enlargement of branch showing recurved branch tip.

Galaxaura Lamouroux

Strictly warm-water algae, species of *Galaxaura* are distributed throughout the Caribbean and along the coasts of Central and South America. Several species occur along the Florida coast but none, so far as is known, are to be found further north.

Superficially resembling small corals in both size and appearance, these bushy little plants are frequently highly colored, from bright orange to rusty red or pale pink. The axes branch dichotomously and may be soft textured and covered with fine delicate hairs, or the branches may be smooth and wiry with some calcification. Attachment, usually to rocks, shell, or coral, is by means of a disc-shaped holdfast.

In size, species of *Galaxaura* range in height from 2 to 5 inches, seldom taller. If covered with hairs the alga, when submersed, may appear more animal than plantlike. When calcified the plants could be mistaken for pieces of living coral. Close inspection, however, reveals the filamentous construction of the thallus, and membership in the plant kingdom is immediately evident.

These algae are commonly found in shallow water but have been dredged from depths greater than 25 fathoms. There are many unanswered questions concerning the life cycles of these seaweeds.

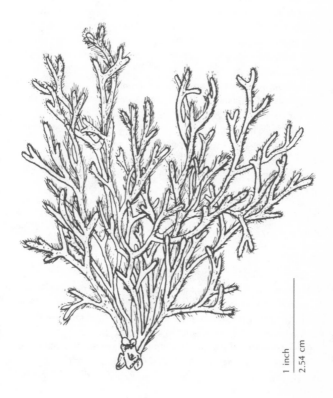

1 inch
2.54 cm

Galaxaura species—the dichotomous branching is characteristic.
The fine delicate hairs, as seen in this species, may or may not be
present.

Corallina officinalis L.   Common Coralline

The deposition of calcium and magnesium carbonates by marine algae is rather common, especially among tropical genera. But just how or why certain seaweeds calcify while others growing nearby do not remains a botanical enigma. It would seem that the deposition of a limestone covering would effectively serve as a light shield and work to the disadvantage of a photosynthetic plant unless the light were so intense that screening became a necessity. But this certainly is not the case with *C. officinalis*, a highly calcified alga which is quite common along the New England coast where light, if anything, is sometimes limiting.

Equally puzzling is the mechanism controlling the lime deposition. *Corallina officinalis* does not incrust indiscriminately. The alga is composed of calcified segments joined together by noncalcified joints. The construction effectively permits the thallus to bend with the current and yield to the surging waves which otherwise would quickly shatter the plant. A number of other calcifying algae are similarly constructed.

The calcified segments of *C. officinalis* are distinctive in their shape and this feature, along with the uncalcified joints, permits quick and easy identification. The plants grow erect from spreading basal discs. The upright axes branch freely and pinnately, usually in one plane. The calcified segments are cylindrical to fan-shaped and arranged in filamentous series. Individual plants may reach a height of 3 to 4 inches. Color varies from purple-red to pale pink. Fragments washed up on the beach are eventually bleached white and if mounted on black paper and framed make interesting arrangements.

Corallina officinalis extends from the Carolinas to Newfoundland, the alga being most abundant in northern waters. Tide pools generally have growths of common coralline, although the plant is known to occur in deep water. Mussels, small stones, and pieces of shells are often colonized.

Corallina cubensis (Montagne) Kützing, another species, is found from North Carolina southward, growing in shallow waters of the intertidal zone. It differs from *C. officinalis* in being irregularly branched with elongated main axis segments and tapered branches. The plants grow erect but reach a height of no more than 1 to 1½ inches.

Toward the end of the eighteenth century, species of *Corallina* were used for medical purposes, extracts of the alga supposedly containing an effective vermifuge. The heavy deposition of calcium carbonate probably curtails the use of coralline algae as a source of food for marine animals.

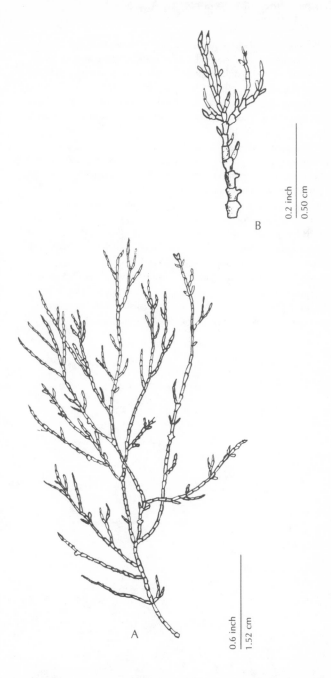

0.2 inch
0.50 cm

B

0.6 inch
1.52 cm

A

Corallina officinalis—(A) habit sketch of plant; (B) an enlargement of axis showing the shapes exhibited by the calcified segments.

Halymenia floresia (Clemente) C. Agardh

This foliaceous to somewhat bushy red alga is common to the shores of southern Florida where it is most frequently encountered as drift, having been washed ashore from the depths. It is a delicate seaweed, gelatinous in texture and soft to the touch. The color varies from a subdued pink to reddish purple depending upon the length of time the plant has been free-floating. The species is one of several of the genus found in Florida waters.

Individual plants may reach a length of 12 to 14 inches and a width of nearly one foot. The main axis is somewhat flattened with numerous side branches, which in turn branch rather profusely. The branches are for the most part opposite each other in arrangement, with the lesser branches toothlike in appearance. Because of the attractive color, gelatinous texture, and foliar nature of the thallus, the alga is easily mounted on herbarium paper or cardboard and makes attractive pictures. As with most red algae, however, the color fades with time, especially if exposed to sunlight.

As a food source for marine animals, little is known about the extent to which species of *Halymenia* are eaten. Quite likely they are consumed by smaller fish and invertebrates. In the Philippine Islands *H. formosa* Harv. is reportedly eaten by humans.

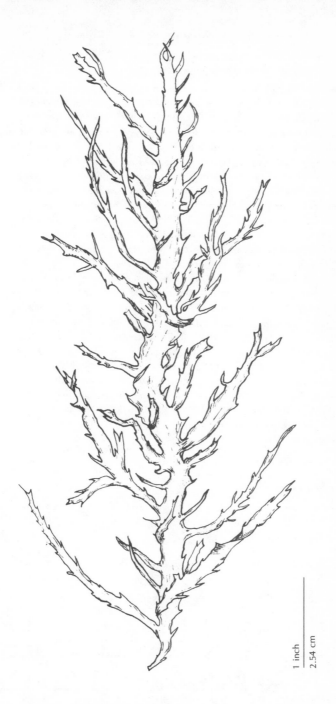

1 inch

2.54 cm

Halymenia floresia—the flat main axis and numerous side branches are distinctive of the species.

Chondrus crispus Stackhouse — Irish Moss, Black Moss, Carrageen

Irish moss is a perennial seaweed which grows attached to rocks from low-tide level to depths of 3 or more fathoms. It is a bushy, dichotomously branched alga composed of many blades which taper toward a disc-shaped holdfast. Each blade is flat, mostly in one plane, somewhat cartilaginous and often crisped at the tips. Individual plants may reach a height of 6 inches and a breadth of 4 or more inches. The plants generally grow in such dense colonies that rocks below low-tide level often appear to be completely covered with a never-ending population. Color varies from deep reddish purple, almost black tones in shaded or deep growing plants, to a yellow-green or pinkish green color in plants exposed to strong light. Drift specimens bleach white or, if left to dry quickly in the sun, turn black. This alga is geographically distributed from New Jersey northward, becoming especially abundant north of Cape Cod.

Black moss is commercially harvested in the Maritime Provinces and certain areas of New England. The harvested alga is dried, sometimes bleached, baled, and shipped to processors who produce a marketable extract known as carrageenin. The extract, a gelatinous carbohydrate from the cell walls, is used extensively as a stabilizer or emulsifier in the production of dairy products, baked goods, pharmaceuticals, and cosmetics. It is also used for clarifying beer, sizing cloth, tanning leather, paper making, paint manufacture, fish packing, and meat canning. The uses of the product seem almost endless with demands for carrageenin increasing annually. The future of the Irish moss industry looks very promising as long as supply and demand are kept in balance through controlled harvesting and conservation.

Chondrus crispus—(A) habit sketch of alga growing on a rock; (B, C) variations in blades.

Gracilaria verrucosa (Hudson) Papenfuss

Of the dozen or more species of Gracilaria known to occur in southern waters, G. verrucosa is one of the more conspicuous and probably one of the most common. Its size, up to 12 inches or more, its purple-red to wine red color, and its cylindrical tapered branches, noticeably narrowed at their base, readily catch one's attention. Rather large fragments of the alga are often seen as drift specimens in the shallow waters of protected bays and inlets. In texture, the plant is cartilaginous and somewhat slippery.

The alga is a shallow-water species attached by means of a small disc-shaped holdfast. Drift specimens are unlikely to have holdfasts since they are generally fragments only. Nevertheless, the plants tend to be somewhat bushy, branching freely but sparingly from the point of attachment. The branches are mostly rather long, tapered into fine points, and radially arranged on the main axes which may be close to ⅛ inch in diameter. The branching is alternate throughout, although very small branchlets may appear to be opposite. Distribution extends from Nova Scotia to the Caribbean.

Certain species of Gracilaria are used as food in Japan, Hawaii, and the Philippines, and for the preparation of pharmaceuticals in China. Gracilaria verrucosa is used as a source of agar-agar in the United States.

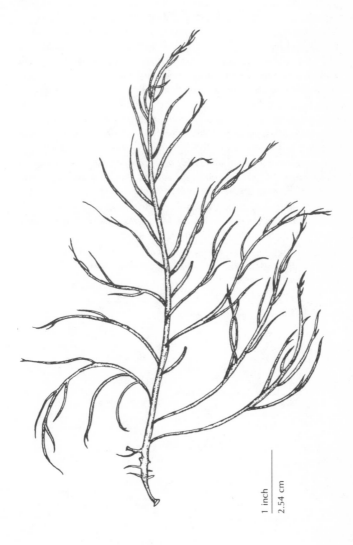

1 inch
2.54 cm

Gracilaria verrucosa—the cylindrical tapered branches, narrowed
at their base, are characteristic.

Grinnellia americana (C. Agardh) Harvey

Color and form alone are sufficient to make this alga one of the most striking and beautiful of all the red seaweeds. However, fruiting specimens become speckled with small dark spots which add to the conspicuousness of the alga and make it even more attractive. The thin, membranous, rosy pink blades, lanceolate to ovate in shape and ruffled at the margins, develop round, smaller than pinhead spots (female plants) or elongated, somewhat irregular and slightly larger spots (spore-bearing plants called tetrasporophytes) which contrast strongly with the rest of the blade. Male plants are not conspicuously speckled. A prominent, unbranched midrib is exhibited by the blades of all three kinds of plant.

This species is generally attached to small stones and shells by means of a tiny holdfast at the end of a short stalk. There is a tendency for the plants to be gregarious, several blades spreading from what would appear to be a common holdfast. Individual plants may reach a length of 1 to 2 feet with a blade 2 to 4 inches broad. The alga grows rapidly, appearing suddenly during midsummer and disappearing just as rapidly several weeks later. At times, masses of the seaweed occur as drift, especially in early August along the shores of Rhode Island and Long Island Sound. Geographically, *Grinnellia* ranges from the Carolinas to northern Massachusetts.

Economically, this seaweed is not important, although it is probably eaten by fish and invertebrates. Artistically, it can be used effectively for making Christmas cards and pictures or for decorating stationery, since the blades stick readily to heavy paper or cardboard. The thallus fades quickly, however, in strong light.

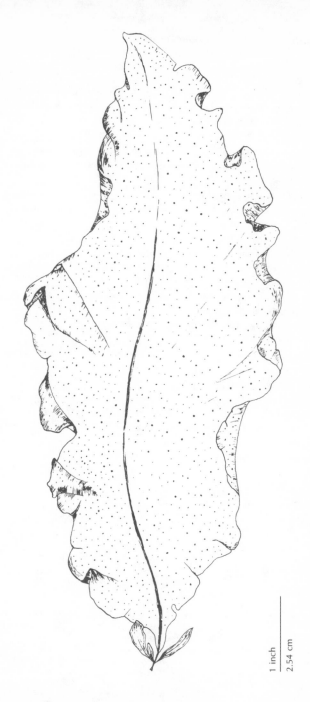

Grinnellia americana—habit sketch of entire plant showing the tiny holdfast, unbranched midvein, and membranous form.

1 inch

2.54 cm

Agardhiella tenera (J. Agardh) Schmitz

Two species of *Agardhiella* are found along our Atlantic coast but only one, *A. tenera*, is of such common occurrence as to be included in this manual. It is a bushy, shallow-water alga found in quiet waters just below low-tide level. The range of the seaweed extends from the tropics to New Hampshire, but the alga is of rare occurrence north of Cape Cod. *Agardhiella ramosissima* (Harvey) Kylin, the other species, is found from North Carolina south and is a deep-water seaweed occasionally dredged from considerable depths.

Agardhiella tenera may form very dense colonies completely covering rocks and boulders in quiet inlets and bays. The fleshy thallus reaches a height of 12 or more inches and is usually a deep rosy red color with tinges of yellowish green. Its dense bushy form makes it ideal for harboring and protecting small fishes and invertebrates.

Growth is from a disc-shaped to somewhat fibrous holdfast, the main axis branching irregularly and profusely with the larger branches reaching a size comparable to the main axis and sometimes making the latter hard to distinguish. The thallus is cylindrical throughout in contrast to the compressed branches of *A. ramosissima*. In both species the branches are constricted at their base.

Agardhiella closely resembles *Gracilaria* in both texture and form. Only microscopic examination of sections of the axis make positive identification of nonfruiting specimens possible, although subtle differences in coloring and branching are apparent to the specialist. Large specimens of *A. tenera* are hefty and seemingly top-heavy when removed from the water, but it must be noted that this feature is also characteristic of some species of *Gracilaria*.

1 inch
2.54 cm

Agardhiella tenera—habit sketch of whole plant showing mode of branching, tapered apices, and disc-shaped holdfast.

Rhodymenia palmata (L.) Greville   Dulse

A cup of soup and a sandwich in some restaurants along the coast of Nova Scotia is often accompanied by several pieces of dried *Rhodymenia palmata*. The alga is eaten like potato chips or chewed like gum depending upon one's likes or dislikes. In Scotland and the Maritime Provinces of Canada the seaweed is known as "dulse." In Ireland it goes by the name "dillisk," and in Iceland it is known as "sol." It has been used as food for centuries, but the flavor is distinctly a "taste of the sea" and is disagreeable to most inlanders. In Nova Scotia and New Brunswick dulse is marketed in small cellophane packages, sold by the can, and in some grocery stores in bulk by the pound.

Rhodymenia palmata ranges from New Jersey northward to Newfoundland and Ellesmere Island. It becomes common north of Cape Cod, growing best in colder waters, and can be found the year around, from the intertidal zone into deep water.

The thallus consists of a flat, often mitten-shaped blade and a very short stalk. Attachment to rocks and shells is by means of a small disclike holdfast. Individual plants may reach a length of 15 to 20 inches with blades 6 or more inches broad. Color ranges from deep red to purple to almost black. Not infrequently, smaller blades develop along the margin of the main blade, which with age becomes divided into broad segments. These features, combined with a slippery, somewhat leathery texture, facilitate ready identification.

The nutritive value of dulse is low since the human digestive system cannot utilize many of the carbohydrates found in seaweeds. As a source of vitamins and trace elements, however, dulse is probably of some value. Regardless, those who have acquired the taste for seaweed are, no doubt, little concerned about nutritive value and eat it simply because they like it or because it has always been a part of their diet.

1 inch
2.54 cm

Rhodymenia palmata—habit sketch of a plant attached to a mussel. The small blades on the margin of the main blade are typical.

Bostrychia montagnei Harvey

Dense colonies of this shaggy, feathery alga may completely cover the stilt roots of red mangrove plants (*Rhizophora Mangle* L.) which line the salt and brackish shores of the Florida peninsula and the Florida Keys. Protected from excessive light and desiccation at low tide by the overhanging branches of the almost impenetrable mangrove jungles, the alga grows profusely forming lush shelter for myriads of small animals. Some probably feed on the branches of the alga, although the plants in general are somewhat coarse and stiff.

Color varies from yellow-green to reddish purple depending upon light intensity and length of time exposed to drying during low tide. The thallus attaches to the mangrove root by means of rhizoidal holdfasts and may be several inches in breadth spreading radially from the point of attachment. Branches are alternately arranged with the smaller, softer branchlets conspicuously incurved. The lower portions of main branches tend to be sparsely branched or bare.

The geographical range of *B. montagnei* extends south from Florida into the Caribbean, the species restricted almost entirely to growing on red mangrove roots in shallow water and shady habitats. One species, *B. radicans* Mont., is consumed as food in Burma.

Bostrychia montagnei—(A) habit sketch of alga growing on mangrove stilt root; (B) one branch, natural size; (C) enlargement of branch to show feathery, incurved branchlets.

Bryothamnion triquetrum (Gmelin) Howe

The specific epithet, *triquetrum*, refers to the triangular-shaped branches of this tropical alga. Growing in shrublike masses on rocks in shallow water, the thallus may reach a height of 8 to 12 inches and a breadth of 6 inches or more. Spreading from a somewhat rubbery disc-shaped holdfast, the cylindrical main axes branch freely and irregularly. The branches are distinctly triangular in shape, due in part to short, stubby branchlets which clothe the upper parts of both major and minor axes. The branchlets tend to be forked at their tips. The plant is cartilaginous in texture and ranges from dull reddish brown to a deep wine color.

The alga is strictly a warm-water seaweed, its distribution extending from Florida southward. In addition to providing convenient shelter to small marine fauna, it likely serves as food for some fishes and invertebrates, since the axes and branches are rather fleshy. No use to man has been reported, although aesthetically the plant is a valuable addition to the marine flora and tropical algal community.

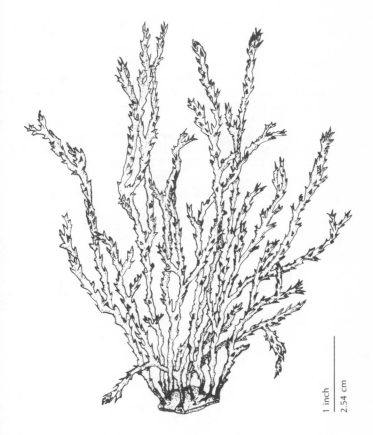

1 inch

2.54 cm

Bryothamnion triquetrum—the bushy growth form, triangular-shaped branches, and forked branch tips are characteristic of the species.

Ceramium rubrum (Hudson)   Pottery Seaweed
C. Agardh

As many as 14 species of the genus *Ceramium* are to be found along the
Atlantic coast. They are separated on the basis of microscopic features and
are a challenge even to the professional botanist. Fortunately, identification of the genus is not as difficult as the identification of a member
species. The branching thallus appears segmented, even without magnification. Under a 10X hand lens the segmentation appears as a distinct
banding of the branches and is due to what the specialist calls cortication.
Coupled with the distinctive banding is a pincherlike or "lobster claw"
appearance of branch tips. Each apex consists of minute, dichotomously
forked, incurved divisions which strongly suggest some type of a grasping
appendage.

Ceramium rubrum is probably the most common species. It is found
from the tropics to Baffin Island and therefore is likely to be found anywhere along the east coast. It may vary in color from any shade of red to
brown to yellow-green and in habit may range from small free-floating
specimens to entangled colonies attached to a variety of substrates. Attachment is by means of a disclike base, the bushy thallus up to a foot in
length but most frequently only several inches long. The alga is rather firm,
almost coarse, with major axes about $1/16$ of an inch thick. Branching is
basically dichotomous, abundant, and tapering.

In Japan, *C. rubrum* is used for the production of Kanten (agar), apparently not extensively for the product is reported to be of inferior quality.
For decorative purposes the alga mounts well and can be used effectively
for Christmas cards, arrangements, stationery, etc. It likewise is probably a
source of food for small fishes and invertebrates.

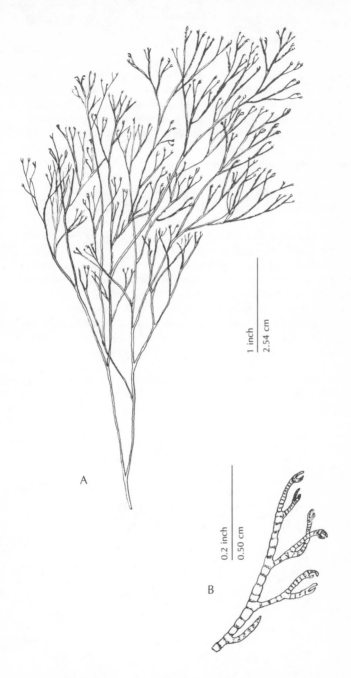

Ceramium rubrum—(A) portion of thallus showing mode of branching and gross form; (B) magnification of branch tips showing clawlike apices and banding of axis.

A

B

1 inch
2.54 cm

0.2 inch
0.50 cm

Dasya pedicellata   Chenille Seaweed
(C. Agardh) C. Agardh

Members of this genus are more at home in the tropics than in the cooler
waters of temperate regions. However, *D. pedicellata* is one species that
has adapted well to temperature extremes and is geographically distributed from the Caribbean to Great Bay, New Hampshire. It characteristically is found in shallow protected waters growing on shells and
stones. Drift fragments are also of common occurrence, particularly in the
wash along the shores of bays and inlets.

In the water, *D. pedicellata* is one of the most beautiful of all seaweeds.
From a single small disc-shaped holdfast there arises a cylindrical central
axis which branches freely, producing many lateral branches. These
branches, as well as the main axis, are clothed with numerous fine hairs,
which give the alga its symmetrical beauty and account for the common
name. Color ranges from a deep wine to reddish pink, not as deeply
colored in the tropics as in northern waters. The thallus may reach a length
of 2 to 3 feet and a breadth of 2 or more feet as the branches spread from
the main axis. Removed from the water, the hairs on the branches mat,
and the alga has a very unattractive, slimy, ropelike appearance.

This particular species of red alga adheres well to paper and retains its
color. Carefully mounted it makes beautiful pictures, Christmas cards,
place mats, etc. It has no other reported economic significance.

1 inch
2.54 cm

Dasya pedicellata—entire plant showing mode of branching, feathery appearance, and small holdfast.

Laurencia papillosa (Forsskål) Greville

Visitors to the beaches of southern Florida are likely to find fragments of this cartilaginous, bushy red alga floating in the surf. It is coarse in texture, much branched and knobby in appearance. The latter feature is distinctive of the species and is due to the numerous short lateral branches which, like the main axis and larger branches, are cylindrical in shape. The alga may reach a length of 6 inches, growing erect from a basal, rhizoidal holdfast. The plant typically grows in the intertidal zone on rocks exposed to the surf. Color varies from dark olive green to greenish purple.

Characteristic of the genus, and barely visible in *L. papillosa* when viewed with a 10X hand lens, is a pit or depression at the apex of each branch. The growing point or apical cell is located at the base of the depression. A slight swelling of the branch tip around the pit forms a collar of tissue which emphasizes the depression.

Several species of *Laurencia* have been reported from as far north as North Carolina, but typically the genus is tropical, being widespread throughout the Caribbean. *Laurencia papillosa* is distributed from Florida south into the tropics.

There are reports that certain species of *Laurencia* are eaten by man in Scotland, the Philippines, New Caledonia, and other Pacific islands. In Hawaii, *L. papillosa* is eaten and referred to as Limu Lipeepee.

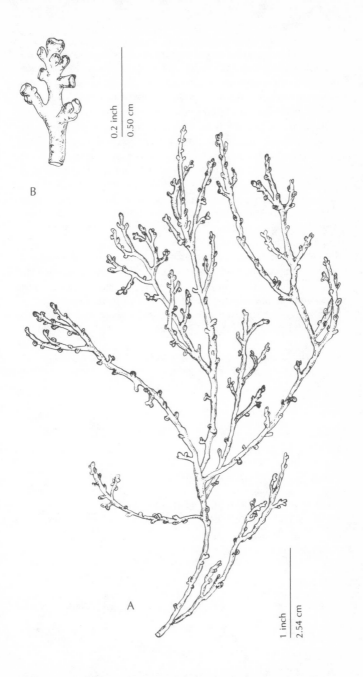

Laurencia papillosa—(A) habit sketch of thallus showing characteristic knobby appearance; (B) magnification of branch tips showing apical pits.

Phycodrys rubens (Hudson) Batters   Sea Oak

One would be hard pressed to find a seaweed—red, brown, or green—more attractive and beautiful than *P. rubens*. The thin, membranous blade, notched at the margin and shaped like an oak leaf, has such a striking resemblance to the oak leaf, even down to the pinnate venation, that the alga is highly prized for making Christmas cards, pictures, and other decorative items. The deep red to rosy pink color, highlighted by the somewhat darker veins, is enough to attract the attention of the most casual observer.

Phycodrys rubens is a deep-water alga distributed from New Jersey north to Ellesmere Island. It becomes common north of Cape Cod growing on rocks, shells, and coarser algae. Attachment is by means of a small, inconspicuous holdfast from which arises a short stalk with one or more blades. Individual plants may reach a length of 6 to 12 inches with blades 3 to 4 inches wide. Fragments of the alga are frequently found in the surf and tidal wash of beaches and coves.

While the typical shape of the blade of *P. rubens* is that of an oak leaf, variations are common and fronds may become elongated and linear. The venation is distinctive, however, and even fragments of the blade will generally show several veins. Thus the alga is easily identified.

Other than decorative purposes, this seaweed has no known economic use. But if beauty alone vindicates existence, then this alga qualifies.

0.5 inch

1.27 cm

Phycodrys rubens—habit sketch of whole plant showing the tiny holdfast, oak leaf appearance of the blade, and venation.

Polysiphonia Greville

The genus *Polysiphonia* is cosmopolitan and one of the most commonly encountered red seaweeds. There are approximately 150 species worldwide, and *in toto* they exhibit adaptation to nearly every conceivable type of marine habitat. Some species are to be found only in deep water, some in tide pools or the shallow waters of quiet lagoons. Some are epiphytic on coarser algae or marine vascular plants. Others are to be found on rocks, shells, or wood pilings. There are free-floating species and species which are to be found only on rocks or jetties facing the open sea and subject to thunderous surf. Many occur in tidal marshes and brackish estuaries. One species is restricted entirely to growth on fucoids.

Because *Polysiphonia* is so common, the genus has been studied thoroughly and the life history is well known, the reproductive cycle often cited as being typical of the division Rhodophycophyta. It is not, but the cycle does exhibit many of the reproductive complexities to be found in red algae as a group.

Species of *Polysiphonia* are separated chiefly on the basis of microscopic features, there being few gross morphological characters helpful in species recognition. Members of the genus can usually be recognized, however, with the aid of a hand lens, although this is not always possible.

The name *Polysiphonia* means "many tubes" or "many siphons" and refers to the structure of the thallus. The main axis and branches of the plant consists of a central filament of cells arranged end to end, with each cell of the series surrounded by four or more lateral cells known as "pericentral cells." The number of pericentral cells, determined by microscopic examination, is critical to the identification of the species. About the most one can hope to determine with a hand lens is whether or not there are pericentral cells present. If so, the branches, particularly the younger parts or branch tips, will appear ribbed (see illustration p. 165) or tubular. Thus the generic name.

Since field identification of species of *Polysiphonia* is next to impossible, no attempt is made in this manual to encompass the two dozen or more species known to occur along the Atlantic coast. Instead, only two are discussed, one because it is so restricted in habitat as to be easily recognized and the other because it is common all along the coast, from Florida to Maine. Examination of either will give the reader an idea of what a species of *Polysiphonia* looks like and precisely what is meant by the term "polysiphonous."

Polysiphonia denudata (Dillwyn) Kützing

This species of *Polysiphonia* may be encountered anywhere along the Atlantic coast, from the tropics to Prince Edward Island. It commonly occurs in tide pools and in warm, shallow bays and inlets growing at-

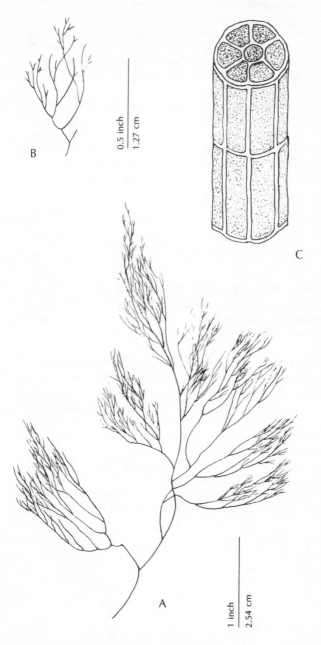

Polysiphonia denudata—(A) habit sketch of thallus showing growth form; (B) enlargement of a small portion of the thallus showing mode of branching; (C) high magnification of plant axis showing polysiphonous arrangement of cells.

tached to rocks, shells, wharfs, and other submerged objects. Frequently it is found growing as an epiphyte on eelgrass (*Zostera marina*).

Color varies from a light pinkish red to purplish red in the uppermost branches on the thallus to a dark red, almost black color at the base. The brushlike branch tips are soft and pliable, and the basal segments tend to be stiff, slender, and sparsely branched. Microscopic examination reveals six pericentral cells.

Individual plants may reach a length of 10 or more inches, wide-spreading from the point of attachment. The alga can be easily mounted for its sticks readily to paper or cardboard. It may therefore be used successfully for pictures or other decorative purposes. The color holds well if the pressed plants are not subjected to lengthy periods of strong light. Quite likely the plant is a source of food for any number of marine animals.

Polysiphonia lanosa (L.) Tandy

This species of *Polysiphonia* is an epiphyte associated with *Ascophyllum nodosum* throughout most of the latter's range and occasionally found on other rockweeds such as *Fucus vesiculosus* and *F. spiralis*. Its restriction to growth on fucoids, in particular *A. nodosum*, makes its identification in the field rather easy.

The alga is deep red, almost black, and forms small bushy outgrowths several inches in diameter on the host weed. Attachment is by means of long unicellular rhizoids with penetrating swollen tips. The thallus tends to be stiff and wiry, the short branches all of nearly equal length giving the plant a near spherical, sheared appearance. Seldom is the alga more than 1 to 1½ inches tall. Viewed under a microscope, the axis is seen to have 20 or more pericentral cells.

It is not completely understood why this alga shows a preference to growth on *Ascophyllum* and other rockweeds. Probably there is a relationship between an ability to withstand desiccation and tolerance to an intertidal habitat, a tolerance not exhibited by most red algae.

1 inch

2.54 cm

Polysiphonia lanosa—habit sketch of alga growing on *Ascophyllum nodosum.*

Field Notes

The Flowering Plants

Division *Anthophyta*

Gr. *anthos*, flower +
phyton, plant

Although there are many flowering plants closely associated with the marine environment, from the mangrove thickets of the tropics to the salt marshes of temperate regions, few qualify as seaweeds in the sense that they grow wholly submerged. Of the latter, commonly known as "sea grasses," there are eight genera embracing some 45 species. Two species are considered common enough along the Atlantic coast to be included in this publication—eelgrass and turtle grass.

The flowering plants, unlike algae, exhibit internal differentiation of tissues to the extent that a complex conducting system known as the vascular cylinder occurs. The cylinder is composed of highly specialized water-conducting cells, collectively known as the xylem, and a combination of cells specialized for food conduction known collectively as the phloem. Extensions of the vascular cylinder are generally visible in the leaves in the form of veins.

In addition to possessing a vascular system, flowering plants reproduce sexually by the formation of seeds, another feature which distinguishes them from algae, and the plant body is generally differentiated into well defined stems, leaves, and roots. As a result, flowering plants in general and the sea grasses in particular can be quickly recognized, even by the nonprofessional. They will not ordinarily be mistaken for any of the algae.

Zostera marina L.   Eelgrass, Barnacle Grass,
                                       Grass Wrack

Eelgrass is geographically distributed along the Atlantic coast from south-
west Greenland to South Carolina. It is characteristically found in shallow
lagoons and protected bays but also occurs in waters deep enough for
dredging. In areas of abundance it forms extensive "grass beds" which
support a wide variety of animals, from migrating birds to numerous invertebrates and fishes. The importance of these beds to wildlife survival was
not fully realized until a mysterious disease known as "wasting disease"
struck in 1931. Within a few years the beds began to disappear, the
shellfish industry began to suffer, and a crisis appeared imminent. Fortunately, the disease declined before the beds were wiped out completely,
and the grass has made a steady comeback, much to the relief of commercial fishermen and conservationists. Nevertheless, the decaying accumu-
lations of eelgrass on beaches following storms is enough to cause some
coastal residents to regard the grass as a nuisance rather than an important
and necessary component of the seaweed flora. It is hoped that these
people will someday come to realize the importance of this plant.

The leaves of *Z. marina* are linear, up to 3 feet in length and ¼ inch
wide. Three, sometimes five, principal veins run the length of the blade.
On living, healthy plants the leaves are green. They turn black when dead
and may bleach white when cast up on the beach. They grow in clumps
from a knobby, stoloniferous rhizome which attaches to the muddy or
sandy substrate by numerous adventitious roots. Flowers are small and
inconspicuous. Seeds are strongly ribbed and also quite small, less than ⅛
inch in length and oval shaped. Geese, ducks, and brant feed on the seeds
as do some fish. A number of epiphytic algae colonize the leaves, and
colonies of bottom floating algae often grow in tangled masses among the
grass clumps (see p. 15).

2 inches
5.08 cm

Zostera marina—habit sketch of plant showing knobby rhizome, adventitious roots, and linear leaves.

Thalassia testudinum Koenig & Sims　　　　　Turtle Grass

The most abundant sea grass in the tropical Western Atlantic region, turtle grass extends from eastern Florida, near Vero Beach, south into the Caribbean, around the southern tip of Florida and along the entire coast of the Gulf of Mexico to southern Texas. Like eelgrass, the plant is chiefly an inhabitant of shallow bays, lagoons, and inlets, forming extensive grassy meadows which shelter a variety of animals. The herbivorous green turtle feeds on the grass, and starfish, sea urchins, loggerhead sponges, sea biscuits, sea fans, soft corals, sea pens, and conchae are to be found within the beds.

From extensive, creeping rhizomes buried in the sand and mud, strap-shaped leaves, up to a foot in length and ½ inch broad, develop in clumps. The leaves are dark green, blunt at the tip, and usually encrusted with epiphytes and calcareous deposits. One main vein and several small veins run the length of the blade. The leaf clusters are sheathed at the base and the rhizome is somewhat hairy with coarse, fibrous, adventitious roots developing at the nodes.

In Florida, flowering occurs between May and July. The flowers, like those of eelgrass, are unisexual. When present they are fairly conspicuous, especially the staminate flower which is produced on a long stalk. Pistillate flowers are sessile and produce pointed, oval-shaped fruits containing numerous seeds.

2 inches
5.08 cm

Thalassia testudinum—habit sketch of plant with staminate flower (a).

Field Notes

Animals That Look Like Plants

Submerged and undisturbed, a number of marine invertebrates might be mistaken for plants. This resemblance is reflected in the names given to some of the groups to which they belong—the Anthozoa or flowerlike animals and the Bryozoa or mosslike animals. The familiar "Air Fern," also known as "Neptune Fern," "Aqua Fern," and "Magic Fern," now being sold in many department stores, novelty shops, and even by some seed companies, is a coelenterate, *Sertularia argentea* L. It is sometimes advertised as a "rare fern" from the bottom of the English Channel that will add a decorative touch to a bouquet or planter and needs no water or fertilizer to grow. Decorative it is, but being the remains of a dead animal it will not grow, no matter what, although in high humidity it may expand and appear to have grown. The green color is due to a dye or paint that is used to color the skeleton.

Sea fans, sea whips, sea feathers, sea pens, sea anemones, and some corals, in addition to bryozoans, may superficially resemble plants. The extended tentacles of these animals when they are submerged gives them a soft textured appearance, and the ramifications of the body skeleton add to the illusion. Washed up on the beach, these organisms can generally be quickly recognized for what they are, either because of the hard skeleton or the soft flesh. But some of the bryozoans might easily be mistaken for algae unless scrutinized with a hand lens or a microscope. Then the closely aligned zooids give them away.

Since some of these invertebrates might be found on the beach, particularly in Florida, and in almost every coastal curio shop, a brief description of several of them, along with illustrations of their basic form and structure, follows. If encountered, they should not fool the user of this guide for long, even if the specimen in hand is a different species than described. The structure of all bryozoans is essentially the same, and anthozoans with skeletons will be recognized because of their hard, almost stonelike, skeletal framework.

Bryozoa

Amathia convoluta Lamouroux and   Moss Animals
Bugula turrita (Desor)

There are about 4,000 species of these small colonial animals. They are mainly marine, occurring everywhere in the oceans from the tropics to the polar regions and from the intertidal zone to great depths. Only a few freshwater species are known, but fossil bryozoans number over 15,000 indicating a long lineage for the group as a whole.

The bryozoan colony is generally attached and frequently encrusting. The erect branching colonies are the ones most likely to be mistaken for plants. The individuals making up a colony are small, about 1 millimeter in length, and are known as zooids. Each zooid is composed of two parts, a body wall, or zooecium, and a retractable, tentacled fleshy portion known as the polypide. Dead bryozoans found on the beach are the skeletal remains of the zooids, usually consisting of only the zooecia, but if relatively fresh, polypides may be present and their demise will soon be detected by one's nostrils.

The identification of bryozoans is based upon growth habit and degree of calcification followed by the use of microscopic features, particularly the shape, size, and arrangement of the zooids. In *Amathia convoluta*, for example, the zooids are spirally arranged. In *Bugula turrita*, the zooids are in rows of two. In both species the colony is erect, bushy, and 4 or more inches in height. Color varies from light yellow to orange or brown. Other bryozoans exhibit colors of bright red to wine to varying shades of orange-yellow.

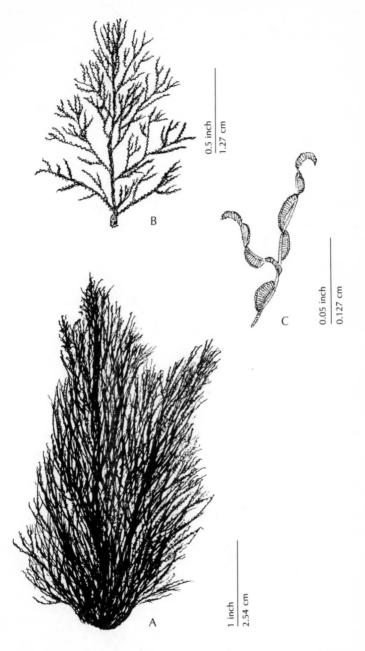

Amathia convoluta—(A) habit sketch of colony showing bushy growth form; (B) portion of colony showing corkscrew appearance of branches; (C) magnification of branch showing the spirally arranged zooids.

0.5 inch
1.27 cm

0.05 inch
0.127 cm

1 inch
2.54 cm

Bugula turrita—(A) habit sketch of colony growing on a shell; (B) branch of colony showing twisted appearance of axes; (C) magnification of branch showing the two-ranked zooids.

Anthozoa

Gorgonia flabellum and
Leptogorgia virgulata (Lamarck)

Flower Animals,
Gorgonians

There are more than 6,000 species in the class Anthozoa of the phylum *Cnidaria*. The sea anemones, sea fans, sea whips, sea feathers, sea pens, and corals are perhaps the better known members. Sea fans, sea whips, and stony corals are commonly for sale in souvenir stands along the coast. The sea fan in particular is sold for decorative purposes.

Members of the class may be solitary or colonial, with or without a skeleton. The skeleton may be massive and stonelike, as in some corals, or composed of internal spicules. Those most likely to be mistaken for plants are the gorgonians or horny corals, the graceful forms of which exhibit a multitude of colors with yellow, orange, red, and purple being common.

Gorgonians occur in all seas but seem to prefer the warmer latitudes. They are abundant in the Indo-Pacific Ocean and the subtropical Atlantic. Those found in souvenir stands and shell shops along the east coast most likely came from the Caribbean—Bermuda, the West Indies, the Bahamas.

The sea fan and a sea plume are illustrated. In both, the skeleton is much branched, the branches all in one plane and anastomosed in *Gorgonia flabellum*, while those of *Leptogorgia virgulata* are multifarious. Tiny openings visible in the skeleton indicate the former position of the living polyps.

Gorgonians may reach a height and breadth of 10 feet. Their spectacular color and plantlike form add much to the beauty of a coral reef. The economically important red coral, *Corallium rubrum* Lam., from the Mediterranean and Japan, is used for making coral jewelry.

181

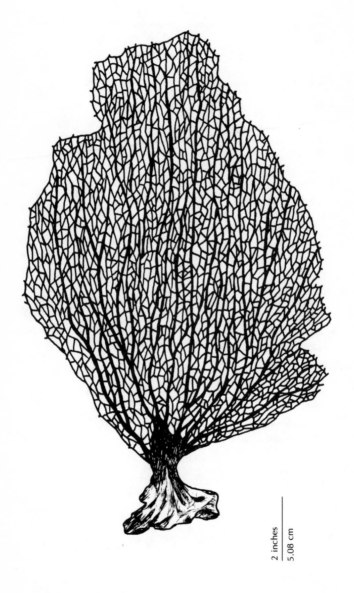

Gorgonia flabellum—whole colony showing anastomosing branches and massive holdfast.

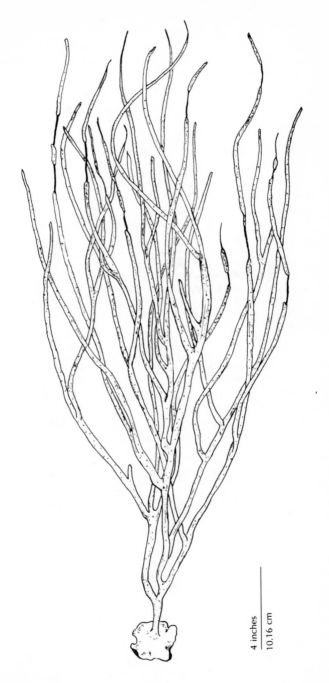

Leptogorgia virgulata—whole colony showing cylindrical branches, mode of branching, and holdfast.

4 inches
10.16 cm

References

Bauchsbaum, Ralph. 1948. *Animals Without Backbones*. Chicago: University of Chicago Press. 405 pp.

Chapman, V.J. 1950. *Seaweeds and Their Uses*. London: Methuen. 287 pp.

Chase, F.M. 1941. *Useful Algae*. Washington, D.C.: Smithsonian Institution publication 3667. 60 pp.

Dawson, E. Yale. 1956. *How to Know the Seaweeds*. Dubuque, Iowa: Wm. C. Brown Co. 197 pp.

———. 1966. *Marine Botany*. New York: Holt, Rinehart and Winston. 371 pp.

Fritsch, F.E. 1935. *The Structure and Reproduction of the Algae*. Vol. I. London: Cambridge University Press. 791 pp.

———. 1945. *The Structure and Reproduction of the Algae*. Vol. II. London: Cambridge University Press. 937 pp.

Gosner, Kenneth L. 1971. *Guide to Identification of Marine and Estuarine Invertebrates*. New York: Wiley. 693 pp.

Hyman, L.H. 1940. *The Invertebrates: Protozoa Through Ctenophora*. New York: McGraw-Hill. 726 pp.

Kingsbury, John M. 1969. *Seaweeds of Cape Cod and the Islands*. Chatham, Mass.: Chatham Press. 212 pp.

Levring, Tore, Heinz A. Hoppe, and Otto J. Schmidt. 1969. *Marine Algae: A Survey of Research and Utilization*. Hamburg: Cram, DeGruyter & Co. 421 pp.

MacFarlane, Constance I. 1956. *Irish Moss in the Maritime Provinces*. Halifax, Nova Scotia: Nova Scotia Research Foundation. 20 pp.

Miner, Roy Waldo. 1950. *Field Book of Seashore Life*. New York: Putnam. 888 pp.

Prescott, G.W. 1968. *The Algae: A Review*. Boston: Houghton Mifflin. 436 pp.

Smith, Gilbert M. 1951. *Manual of Phycology*. Waltham, Mass.: Chronica Botanica. 375 pp.

Taylor, William Randolph. 1957. *Marine Algae of the Northeastern Coast of North America*. Ann Arbor: University of Michigan Press. 509 pp.

———. 1960. *Marine Algae of the Eastern Tropical and Subtropical Coasts of the Americas*. Ann Arbor: University of Michigan Press. 870 pp.

Thorson, Gunnar. 1971. *Life in the Sea*. New York: McGraw-Hill. World University Library. 256 pp.

Tressler, Donald K. 1951. *Marine Products of Commerce*. New York: Reinhold. 782 pp.

Uphof, J.C. Th. 1968. *Dictionary of Economic Plants*. New York: Lehre J. Cramer; Stechert-Hafner Service Agency. 591 pp.

Usher, George. 1974. *A Dictionary of Plants Used by Man*. London: Constable. 619 pp.

Zeiller, Warren. 1974. *Tropical Marine Invertebrates of Southern Florida and the Bahama Islands*. New York: Wiley. 132 pp.

Index / Glossary

ACCESSORY PIGMENT: Light-absorbing pigment indirectly involved in photosynthesis.

Acetabularia crenulata Lamouroux, 52, **53**

ADVENTITIOUS ROOT: A root originating from stem or leaf tissue.

Agardhiella ramosissima (Harvey) Kylin, 148

Agardhiella tenera (J. Agardh) Schmitz, 148, **149**

Agarum cribrosum (Mertens) Bory, 94, **95**

AIR FERN: An invertebrate animal currently being sold as an ornamental plant.

Alaria esculenta (L.) Greville, 96, **97**

ALGIN: Soluble sodium salt of alginic acid, a cell wall component of brown algae.

ALGINATES: The salts of alginic acid of commercial importance.

Amathia convoluta Lamouroux, 178, **179**

ANASTOMOSED: Connected.

Animals that look like plants, 177

ANNUAL: A plant which completes its life cycle within one growing season.

ANTHOPHYTA: The flowering plants, 171

ANTHOZOA: Flowerlike animals; a class of invertebrates in the phylum Cnidaria, 181

APICAL CELL: Single cell at the apex of a plant axis which, by cell division, adds to the length of the axis.

APICULATE: Ending abruptly in a sharp point.

AQUA FERN: Another name for Air Fern.

ARTICULATED: Jointed or appearing jointed.

Ascophyllum nodosum (L.) Le Jolis, 112, **113**

Asparagopsis hamifera (Hariot) Okamura, 134, **135**

Asparagopsis sanfordiana Harv., 134

Avrainvillea longicaulis (Kützing) Murray & Boodle, 20, **21**

AXIAL: Relating to the plant axis.

AXIAL CELL: A cell within, or a part of, the plant axis.

AXIAL FILAMENT: A chain of cells or an elongated cell of the plant axis.

BARNACLE GRASS: *Zostera marina*.

Batophora oerstedi J. Agardh, 54, **55**

BLACK MOSS: *Chondrus crispus*.

BLACK TANG: *Fucus vesiculosus*.

BLADDER FUCUS: *Fucus vesiculosus*.

BLADDER WRACK: *Fucus vesiculosus*.

BOREAL: Related to or located in northern regions.

Bostrychia montagnei Harvey, 152, **153**

Bostrychia radicans Mont., 152

BRACKISH: Somewhat salty; referring to a mixture of saltwater and freshwater.

BRANCHLET: A small branch; the ultimate division of a branch.

BROADLEAF KELP: *Laminaria saccharina*.

BROWN ALGAE: Members of the division Phaeophycophyta.

Bryopsis plumosa (Hudson) C. Agardh, 22, **23**

Bryothamnion triquetrum (Gmelin) Howe, 154, **155**

BRYOZOA: A phylum of invertebrates, 178

BRYOZOAN: A member of the phylum Bryozoa.

Bugula turrita (Desor), 178, **180**

CALCAREOUS: Calcified.

CALCIFIED: Covered by or impregnated with calcium salts.

CARRAGEEN: *Chondrus crispus*.

CARRAGEENAN: A gelatinlike substance derived from *Chondrus crispus* and other red algae. Same as CARRAGEENIN.

CARRAGEENIN: See CARRAGEENAN.

CARTILAGINOUS: Firm but rubbery; flexible.

Caulerpa Lamouroux, 24

Caulerpa mexicana (Sonder) J. Agardh, 24, **25**

Caulerpa paspaloides (Bory) Greville, 26, **27**

Caulerpa prolifera (Forsskål) Lamouroux, 28, **29**

Caulerpa sertularioides (Gmeln.) Howe, 30, **31**

Ceramium rubrum (Hudson) C. Agardh, 156, **157**

Chaetomorpha linum (Müller) Kützing, 14, **15**

CHENILLE SEAWEED: *Dasya pedicellata*.

CHLOROPHYCOPHYTA: The division of green algae, 7

Chondrus crispus Stackhouse, 142, **143**

Chorda Stackhouse, 98

Chorda filum (L.) Lamouroux, 98, **99**

186 *Chorda tomentosa* Lyngbye, 100, **101**

Cladophora Kützing, 16, **17**

Cladophoropsis membranacea (C. Agardh) Børgesen, 56, **57**

CNIDARIA: The coelenterates; a phylum of invertebrates.

Codium Stackhouse, 32

Codium decortatum (Woodward) Howe, 32

Codium fragile (Suringar) Hariot, 32, **33**

Codium isthmocladum Vickers, 34, **35**

COELENTERATA: A phylum of invertebrates.

COELENTERATE: A member of the phylum Coelenterata.

COENOCYTIC: A multinucleate organism or thallus lacking crosswalls.

COLONIAL: Of or relating to a colony.

COLONY: A group of independent organisms living together.

COMMON CORALLINE: *Corallina officinalis.*

Corallina cubensis (Montagne) Kützing, 138

Corallina officinalis L., 138, **139**

CORALLINE: Calcareous algae; of or resembling coral.

Corallium rubrum Lam: Red coral, 181

CORTICATE: Covered by an outer layer of cells or a partial layer of cells.

CORTICATING: Cells or filaments which cover or partially cover the axis of a thallus.

CRISPED: Curly; roughened into small folds or wrinkles.

CRYPTOSTOMATA: Cavities containing tufts of hairs.

CUNEATE: Wedge-shaped; triangular.

Dasya pedicellata (C. Agardh) C. Agardh, 158, **159**

Dasycladus vermicularis (Scopoli) Krasser, 58, **59**

DEAD MAN'S FINGERS: *Codium fragile.*

DECIDUOUS: Falling off; not persistent.

Desmotrichum undulatum (J. Agardh) Reinke, 88, **89**

DEVIL'S SHOELACE: *Chorda filum.*

DICHOTOMOUS: Branching in pairs; forked.

Dictyopteris membranacea (Stackhouse) Batters, 74, **75**

Dictyosphaeria cavernosa (Forsskål) Børgesen, 60, **61**

Dictyota ciliolata Kützing, 76, **77**

DILLISK: Irish name for *Rhodymenia palmata.*

DISTALLY: Toward the apex.

DIVISION: A taxonomic category or group of plants.

DULSE: *Rhodymenia palmata.*

Ectocarpus Lyngbye, 68

Ectocarpus confervoides (Roth) Le Jolis, 68, **69**

Ectocarpus dasycarpus Kuckuck, 70, **71**

ECOTYPE: A species variant; a subspecies.

ECOTYPIC: Of or relating to ecotype.

EELGRASS: *Zostera marina.*

Elachistea fucicola (Velley) Areschoug, 82, **83**

Elachistea minutissima Taylor, 82

Enteromorpha intestinalis (L.) Link, 8, **9**

EPIPHYTE: Growing upon but not parasitizing another plant.

EPITHET: A characterizing word or phrase.

FILAMENT: A threadlike cell or chain of cells.

FILAMENTOUS: Composed of filaments; threadlike.

FLOWER-ANIMALS: Members of the Anthozoa.

FLOWERING PLANTS: Members of the division Anthophyta; plants which produce flowers.

FOLIACEOUS: Leaflike.

FRUITING: In vascular plants the production of fruits; in algae the formation of reproductive areas.

FUCOID: Relating to rockweeds; a rockweed.

FUCOXANTHIN: Predominant pigment in brown algae.

Fucus Linnaeus, 114

Fucus edentatus De la Pylaie, 114, **115**

Fucus spiralis L., 116, **117**

Fucus vesiculosus L., 118, **119**

Galaxaura Lamouroux, 136, **137**

GAMETANGIUM (GAMETANGIA, pl.): Cell which produces gametes.

GAMETE: Sex cell or germ cell.

GENUS (GENERA, pl.): A category of biological classification made up of species; the first name in a binomial.

GLABROUS: Smooth.

GLOSSY: Shiny, having a luster.

Gorgonia flabellum L., 181, **182**

GORGONIAN: Certain members of the Anthozoa.

Gracilaria verrucosa (Hudson) Papenfuss, 144, **145**

GRASS WRACK: *Zostera marina.*

GREEN ALGAE: Members of the division Chlorophycophyta; algae in which the predominant pigment is chlorophyll.

GREEN BUBBLE ALGA: *Dictyosphaera cavernosa.*

GREGARIOUS: Tending to associate with others of the same kind; to group.

Grinnellia americana (C. Agardh) Harvey, 146, **147**

GULFWEED: Species of *Sargassum.*

GYMNOSPERM: Cone-bearing seed plant.

HAITA: Chinese name for dried kelp.

Halimeda Lamouroux, 36

Halimeda incrassata (Ellis) Lamouroux, 36, **37**

Halimeda monile (Ellis & Solander) Lamouroux, 38, **39**

Halimeda opuntia (L.) Lamouroux, 40, **41**

Halymenia floresia (Clemente) C. Agardh, 140, **141**

Halymenia formosa Harv., 140

HOLDFAST: Basal cell or organ attaching thallus to the substratum.

HORSETAIL: *Laminaria digitata.*

INTERCALARY: Intermediate; neither basal nor terminal but somewhere between.

INTERSTITIAL: Related to or found in small spaces or cavities; between tissues.

INTERTIDAL: Zone between high and low tide levels.

INVERTEBRATES: Animals without backbones.

IRISH MOSS: *Chondrus crispus.*

KANTEN: A type of agar produced by the Japanese from *Ceramium rubrum.*

KELP: Common name for large brown algae, especially species of *Laminaria.*

KNOBBED WRACK: *Ascophyllum nodosum.*

KNOTTED WRACK: *Ascophyllum nodosum.*

KOMBU: Japanese name for dried kelp marketed for human consumption.

L.: Carolus Linnaeus, a Swedish botanist (1708–1778).

LADY WRACK: Common name for *Fucus vesiculosus.*

LAMINA: Blade; erect flattened portion of thallus; leaflike appendage.

Laminaria Lamouroux, 102

Laminaria agardhii Kjellman, 102, **103**

Laminaria digitata (L.) Lamouroux, 106, **107**

Laminaria longicruris De la Pylaie, 110, **111**

Laminaria platymeris De la Pylaie, 108, **109**

Laminaria saccharina (L.) Lamouroux, 104, **105**

LANCEOLATE: Shaped like a lance; tapering to a point at the apex.

Laurencia papillosa (Forsskål) Greville, 160, **161**

LEAF: In vascular plants, the vascularized appendage originating from the stem; in algae, the flattened part of the axis, leaflike in appearance.

Leathesia difformis (L.) Areschoug, 84, **85**

Leptogorgia virgulata (Lamarck), 181, **183**

Leucobryum glaucum (Hedw.) Ångstr. ex Fr., 56

LIMU KOHU: Hawaiian name for *Asparagopsis sanfordiana*.

LIMU LIPEEPEE: Hawaiian name for *Laurencia papillosa*.

LINK CONFETTI: *Enteromorpha intestinalis*.

MACROSCOPIC: Large enough to be seen with the naked eye.

MAGIC FERN: Another name for Air Fern.

MEMBRANOUS: Thin and sheetlike.

MERMAID'S FAN: Species of *Udotea*.

MERMAID'S WINEGLASS: *Acetabularia crenulata*.

Monostroma oxyspermum (Kützing) Doty, 10, **11**

MOSS ANIMALS: Bryozoans.

MUCILAGE CANAL: A cavity or duct containing mucilage.

MULTICELLULAR: Composed of more than one cell.

MULTIFARIOUS: Diverse; having great variety.

MULTINUCLEATE: Having more than one nucleus or chromosome bearing body.

NEPTUNE FERN: Another name for Air Fern.

NONSEPTATE: Without crosswalls.

OYSTER THIEF: *Codium fragile*.

Padina vickersiae Hoyt, 78, **79**

PELAGIC: Living or occurring in the open sea.

Penicillium: Generic name for the fungus from which the antibiotic penicillin is obtained.

Penicillus Lamarck, 42

Penicillus capitatus Lamarck, 42, **43**

Penicillus dumentosus (Lamouroux) Blainville, 44, **45**

PERENNIAL: A plant that lives for two or more years; requiring more than two years to complete the life cycle.

PERFORATE: Having holes; pierced through.

PERICENTRAL: Lateral to the axial cell.

190 *Petalonia fascia* (O.F. Müller) Küntze, 90, **91**

PHAEOPHYCOPHYTA: The division of brown algae, 67

PHANEROGAM: Seed plant.

PHLOEM: Food-conducting tissue of vascular plant.

PHOTOSYNTHESIS: The manufacture of food from carbon dioxide and water via chlorophyll and light.

PHOTOSYNTHETIC: Capable of photosynthesis.

Phycodrys rubens (Hudson) Batters, 162, **163**

PHYCOLOGY: The study of algae.

PHYLUM: A taxonomic category or group of animals.

PINNA (PINNAE, pl.): Primary division of leaf, branch, or flattened axis.

PINNATE: Arranged on either side of a central strand or axis; featherlike arrangement of parts.

PINNATELY: Arranged in a pinnate fashion.

PINNULE: A secondary pinna.

PISTILLATE FLOWER: Female flower; carpel-bearing flower.

POLYPIDE: The living, fleshy, tentacled part of a zooid.

Polysiphonia denudata (Dillwyn) Kützing, 164, **165**

Polysiphonia Greville, 164

Polysiphonia lanosa (L.) Tandy, 166, **167**

POLYSIPHONOUS: Composed of ''tubes'' or ''siphons.'' See *Polysiphonia*.

Porphyra leucosticta Thuret, 132, **133**

Porphyra umbilicalis (L.) J. Agardh, 132

POTATO CHIP ALGA: *Padina vickersiae*.

POTTERY SEAWEED: *Ceramium rubrum*.

PURPLE LAVER: Species of *Porphyra*.

Pylaiella littoralis (L.) Kjellman, 72, **73**

RACHIS: The axis of a compound appendage or organ.

Ralfsia verrucosa (Areschoug) J. Agardh, 86, **87**

RECEPTACLE: A fertile branch tip bearing cavities in which reproductive cells are produced.

RED ALGAE: Members of the division Rhodophycophyta.

RED LAVER: Species of *Porphyra*.

ROCKWEED: Species of *Fucus;* and a name for *Ascophyllum nodosum*.

ROOT: Lower portion of the vascular plant axis usually serving to anchor the plant in the soil and absorb water and minerals.

Rhipocephalus phoenix (Ellis & Solander) Kützing, 46, **47**

RHIZOID: A unicellular or uniseriate hairlike structure functioning in attachment.

RHIZOIDAL: Pertaining to rhizoids or composed of rhizoids.

RHIZOME: Underground or creeping stem.

Rhizophora Mangle L., 152

RHODOPHYCOPHYTA: The division of red algae, 131

Rhodymenia palmata (L.) Greville, 150, **151**

SARGASSO SEA: An immense lens-shaped mass of floating gulfweed in the North Atlantic, northeast of the West Indies.

Sargassum C. Agardh, 120

Sargassum filipendula C. Agardh, 120, **121**

Sargassum fluitans Bøyesen, 122, **123**

Sargassum natans (L.) J. Meyen, 122, **123**

Sargassum pteropleuron Grunow, 124, **125**

Sertularia argentea L., 177

Scytosiphon lomentaria (Lyngbye) C. Agardh, 92, **93**

SEA COLANDER: *Agarum cribrosum*.

SEA GIRDLE: *Laminaria digitata*.

SEA LETTUCE: *Ulva lactuca*.

SEA OAK: *Phycodrys rubens*.

SEA SAUSAGE: *Scytosiphon lomentaria*.

SEA STAGHORN: *Codium fragile*.

SEA TWINE: *Chorda filum*.

SEA WARE: *Fucus vesiculosus*.

SEA WHISTLE: *Ascophyllum nodosum*.

SEASTAFF: *Laminaria digitata*.

SEED: Reproductive body of phanerogams.

SESSILE: Attached at the base; not stalked.

SHAVING BRUSH ALGA: Species of *Penicillus*.

SOL: Icelandic name for *Rhodymenia palmata*.

SOLITARY: Occurring singly or without companions.

SPAGHETTI GRASS: *Codium fragile*.

SPECIES: A population of plants or animals which maintains distinctness from others; a category of biological classification ranking immediately below genus.

SPICULE: Minute calcareous or siliceous body found in or supporting the tissues of various invertebrates.

Spongomorpha Kützing, 18, **19**

SPORANGIUM (SPORANGIA, pl.): A cell or structure which produces spores.

SPORE: Any of several minute structures, frequently single celled, produced by plants for purposes of reproduction or survival during adverse growing conditions.

SPOROPHYLLS: Fertile leaves.

SPUTNIK WEED: *Codium fragile*.

STAMINATE FLOWER: Male flower; pollen-producing flower.

STEM: The vascularized portion of the plant axis which bears the leaves.

STIPE: Stemlike portion of thallus.

STOLON: Horizontal branch or portion of plant axis usually occurring at ground level and serving purposes of lateral growth.

STOLONIFEROUS: Stolonlike or composed of stolons.

SUBTIDAL: Occurring below low-tide level.

SWEET TANGLE: *Laminaria saccharina*.

TANGLE: *Laminaria digitata* and some other kelps.

TARSPOT: *Ralfsia verrucosa*.

TETRASPOROPHYTE: In red algae, the plant which produces spores having one-half the somatic chromosome number.

Thalassia testudinum Koenig & Sims, 174, **175**

THALLUS (THALLI, pl.): A plant body not highly differentiated; plant lacking true leaves, stems, and roots.

Turbinaria turbinata (L.) Kuntze, 126, **127**

TURTLE GRASS: *Thalassia testudinum*.

Udotea Lamouroux, 48

Udotea flabellum (Ellis & Solander) Lamouroux, 48, **49**

Udotea spinulosa Howe, 50, **51**

Ulva lactuca L., 12, **13**

UNICELLULAR: Composed of a single cell.

UNISEXUAL: Having one sex; producing only male or only female reproductive parts.

UTRICLE: Swollen, bulb-shaped cell found in the thallus of *Codium* species.

Valonia ventricosa J. Agardh, 62, **63**

VASCULAR CYLINDER: Pertaining to the conducting tissues of the plant axis collectively.

VEINS: Strands of conducting tissue in the leaf blade.

VENATION: The arrangement of veins.

VESICLE: An air bladder or fluid-filled sac.

VESICULATE: Of or relating to vesicles.

WASTING DISEASE: A disease which once nearly wiped out the eelgrass beds along the Atlantic coast.

WINGED KELP: *Alaria esculenta*.

XYLEM: Water-conducting tissue of the vascular plant.

YELLOW WRACK: *Ascophyllum nodosum*.

Zonaria tournefortii (Lamouroux) Montagne, 80, **81**

ZONATE: Having distinct zones or regions of specialized cells.

ZOOECIUM: The body wall of a zooid.

ZOOID: The individual in the bryozoan colony.

Zostera marina L., 172, **173**